Betty Crocker's

MEXICAN MADE EASY

MACMILLAN • USA

Macmillan General Reference
A Simon & Schuster Macmillan Company
1633 Broadway
New York, NY 10019-6785

Library of Congress Cataloging-in-Publication Data

Crocker, Betty.
  [Mexican made easy]
  Betty Crocker's Mexican made easy.
    p.   cm.
  Includes index.
  ISBN 0-02-861621-9
    1. Cookery, Mexican.   I. Title.   II. Title: Mexican made easy.
TX716.M4C76   1993
641.5972—dc20   92-25395
                                                       CIP

Designed by Levavi & Levavi
Manufactured in the United States of America

            10 9 8 7 6 5 4 3

Front cover: Mexican Chicken Manicotti (page 33)

Contents

Introduction

Mexican food becomes increasingly popular every day, with more and more people interested in learning about the techniques, tips and ingredients to make great Mexican meals. In this collection you'll find a wide range of Mexican food, from dishes such as tacos, salsa, guacamole and burritos that first came to the American Southwest and then spread throughout the country, to dishes newer to our cuisine, such as hearty Arroz con Pollo and easily assembled Fajitas.

We have also collected recipes that are a happy combination of Mexican and American cooking, among them Taco Salad, Taco Casserole, Mexican Pizza, Sante Fe Flank Steak and Mexican Fried Chicken. These dishes blend classic Mexican spices and flavors with favorites from your own kitchen—a comfortable way to introduce Mexican cooking to family and friends.

You'll find complete and easy-to-understand explanations of Mexican ingredients in the glossary, as well as definitions of different types of Mexican dishes. Whether you are looking up chipotle chiles or wondering what is in a quesadilla, you'll find the information you need right here. Special menus also show you how to use the recipes to plan complete and satisfying meals.

With *Betty Crocker's Mexican Made Easy*, you have everything you need to make preparing Mexican meals a snap. Recipes for appetizers, sauces and sides, main dishes and desserts, as well as clear explanations of ingredients and the Betty Crocker dependability, will make Mexican cooking a pleasurable—and delicious—experience for both beginning and experienced cooks alike.

THE BETTY CROCKER EDITORS

What's What
in Mexican Cooking

Below are definitions of some of the most common dishes found in Mexican cooking. Tortillas, made with corn or flour, are the basis of Mexican meals. They are served as bread, of course, but beyond that they are the definitive ingredient in these Mexican dishes:

- A *burrito* is a flour tortilla folded like an envelope around a filling.
- *Chilaquiles* is a casserole of fried tortilla strips baked with sauces and fillings.
- A *chimichanga* is a *burrito* that traditionally is deep-fat fried after it has been filled.
- An *enchilada* is a filled corn tortilla served with a sauce.
- *Fajitas* are flour tortillas filled with slices of steak, pork, chicken or shrimp and various condiments.
- *Nachos* are crisp chips of corn tortillas served with cheese and salsa or chiles, usually as an appetizer.

- A *quesadilla* is a tortilla, filled principally with cheese, then folded or stacked.
- A *taco* is a tortilla, crisp or soft, folded in half around a filling.

HOW TO USE NUTRITION INFORMATION
Nutrition information per serving for each recipe includes the amounts of calories, protein, carbohydrate, fat, cholesterol and sodium.

- If ingredient choices are given, the first listed ingredient is used in recipe nutrition information calculations.
- When ingredient ranges or more than one serving size is indicated, the first weight or serving is used to calculate nutrition information.
- "If desired" ingredients and recipe variations are not included in nutrition information calculations.

Glossary of Mexican Ingredients

You'll find this glossary helpful when using these recipes.

ADOBO: A piquant sauce of tomato, vinegar and spices.

ANISE SEED: This small, elongated seed tastes sharply of licorice.

AVOCADO: This fruit is ripe when the flesh under the leathery skin yields to light pressure. A hard avocado will ripen if left at room temperature for two or three days. The Haas or California type is smaller and darker green than the emerald type grown in Florida, and some say it is more flavorful as well. Keep avocado flesh from discoloring by brushing it with lemon juice as it is peeled.

BEANS: It takes time to prepare dried beans, but the result is a tender bean that is still firm. Canned beans are sometimes mushy, but they are convenient to keep on hand and are packed in liquid that adds flavor to many recipes. Dried beans keep almost indefinitely. Before cooking dried beans, rinse them well and pick them over for stones or inferior beans.

>   **Black beans** (*frijoles negros*, turtle beans), though small, have a hearty flavor. South American cooking makes great use of them.

With their dramatic dark purple-blue color, they lend themselves nicely to garnishes.

>   **Garbanzo beans** (chickpeas) are Spanish in origin. These rounded, beige beans have a nutty flavor.

>   **Pinto beans** (*frijoles*) are charmingly speckled with brown on a pale or pinkish background.

CAPERS: These are the pickled, green buds from the prickly caper bush. They are somewhat smaller than raisins and are bottled in brine.

CAYENNE: See Chile.

CHEESE: Traditional Mexican cheeses were made with goat's or sheep's milk. The recipes in this book use the following cheeses:

>   **Cheddar** is a mild firm cheese of English origin that becomes more sharp with age. It melts beautifully.

>   **Colby** is a slightly sharp cheese with a flavor similar to that of Cheddar. This American cheese has a rather soft, open texture.

>   **Monterey jack** is a mild cheese usually sold in blocks. It softens at room temperature.

CHILE: Chiles are native to the Americas. They have been known in North America for some time but are said to have traveled north by a circuitous route; they found their way from Mexico to the Western world with Christopher Columbus, then to the East and finally to North America. New strains of chiles are developed frequently, bred for hardiness, sweetness, hotness and so forth. But chiles are full of surprises; two chiles picked from the same plant may vary widely in hotness. To quench the fire of a too-spicy mouthful, do not reach for a water glass. Water will only spread the capsaicin (the compound that our tongues register as "hot") around. Instead, take a large mouthful of something starchy: corn chips, beans, bread or rice. Sometimes finding fresh chiles is difficult. This probably isn't a question of distribution, but of perishability. Canned and dried chiles are usually available.

Anaheim chiles (California green chiles) are slim, between five and eight inches long, and of various light shades of green. These mildly hot chiles are sometimes twisted in appearance. They are occasionally stuffed, but their flesh is thin and more fragile than that of poblano chiles (see right). The Anaheims cultivated in New Mexico—where the name is *chile verde*—are reputedly hotter. A ripe, red Anaheim is sometimes known as a *chile Colorado*. Anaheim chiles are dried and tied in wreathes (*ristras*) and ground and blended in commercial chile powder mixtures. They may be purchased in cans as "mild green chiles." These chiles are named after the town that, at the turn of the century, was the site of a chile cannery.

Ancho refers to a ripened, dried poblano chile.

Cayenne chiles are thin and tapered, three to seven inches long. Dark green (unripe) or bright red (ripe), the cayenne is incendiary and well known to Asian kitchens. The red ones are dried and ground to make cayenne pepper (see, Ground Red Pepper). This product adds heat and just a little chile flavor.

Chipotle chiles are smoked, dried jalapeños with a very wrinkled appearance. Fresh jalapeños are vibrant green but they turn brown when smoked. Chipotles can be purchased loose (dry) or canned in adobo sauce. The canned variety is especially convenient as it saves having to soak and soften them.

Guajillo chiles (mirasol chiles) have a vegetal flavor that shines even through the drying process. Guajillos are orange-red, skinny and about two to three inches long.

Jalapeño chiles range from hot to very hot. They are dark green, fat and about two to three inches long with a characteristically rounded tip. Watch out for the little ones, which are hottest. Jalapeños ripen to red. Use them fresh or pickled.

Poblano is the chile most frequently used for *chiles rellenos*. It is a suave dark green and ranges from mild to hot. Shaped like a long bell pepper, the poblano has a nice shape for stuffing.

Red pepper flakes are just that: flaked, dried ripe chiles. Most red pepper flake mixtures are quite hot.

Serrano chiles are a sort of middling green, developing to brilliant red when ripe. Extremely hot (as hot as any chile), this chile is usually shorter and thinner than the jalapeño.

Roasting chiles: Recipes often call for chiles to be roasted. This enhances the flavor and makes them a snap to peel. Roasted chiles may be frozen before peeling, a convenience if you roast a big batch at once; wrap them airtight in plastic wrap. (See page 12.)

CHILE POWDER: This is a mixture of ground, dried red chiles blended with other spices and herbs. It is said to have been invented by Willie Gebhardt, a Texan, in 1892. Most brands include cumin and oregano. Often chile powder formulas contain paprika, coriander and salt.

Chile powder is not to be confused with ground red chiles.

CHOCOLATE: The Aztecs are credited with the discovery of chocolate. It was probably first used to flavor a bitter drink favored by their mystics. Another Mexican invention, the molinillo, is a wooden whisk used to whip hot chocolate. The handle is rolled between the palms of the hands, whipping the mixture until it is frothy. Today, block Mexican chocolate frequently contains cinnamon, vanilla, clove and ground almonds.

CHORIZO: This spicy smoked pork (or pork and beef) sausage is available both in links and in bulk.

CILANTRO (Mexican parsley. Chinese parsley, fresh coriander): This herb bears a resemblance to flat-leaf parsley, but the flavor is entirely different: strong, fresh, acidic. Cilantro is perishable; store it in the refrigerator with the stems in water and plastic loosely covering the leafy tops.

CINNAMON: This is truly a spice of Mexican cuisine, used in dishes sweet and savory. It is available ground as a powder or in tightly rolled dry quills. Sometimes the bark of the cassia tree is sold as cinnamon; the flavor is similar, but neither as true nor as intense. Look for authentic cinnamon.

CORIANDER: This spice is the seed of the plant that gives us cilantro. It has a dusky flavor that is often associated with Eastern cooking. It may be purchased ground or as whole, dried seeds.

CORN HUSKS: Dried corn husks, softened by soaking, are used to wrap food before it is cooked. They make a sort of natural jacket that holds a mixture together as it steams. Remove any silk clinging to the dried husk before using. Several small corn husks may be overlapped for a larger wrapping, as for a tamale.

CORNMEAL: Dried corn is the staple of Mexican larders. When cornmeal is called for, use yellow or white, coarsely or finely ground.

CUMIN: This is the powerful, sometimes dominating spice so often used in traditional southwest cooking. Recipes may call for whole cumin seed or ground cumin.

GROUND RED CHILES: This is pure chile powder from finely ground, dried red chiles. It is not blended chile powder.

GROUND RED PEPPER: From ground, dried cayenne chiles, this is often called "cayenne pepper." (See Cayenne Chiles.)

INSTANT CORN FLOUR TORTILLA MIX (*masa*): This commercial product is the shortcut in making fresh corn tortillas. It is fresh corn *masa* (see Masa) that has been dried and ground.

JÍCAMA: The flesh of the jícama root is often compared to that of the water chestnut, both for flavor and crunch. Jícama is related to the sharp-tasting turnip but is so mild in flavor that, when eaten raw, it is usually sprinkled with lemon or lime juice and chile powder. After the brown fibrous skin has been pared away, jicama flesh does not discolor. Look for smallish jícama, which will be sweet and moist.

LARD: This has been perhaps the most frequently used cooking fat south of the border since it was introduced by the Spaniards. For tender, flaky pastries, lard can't be beat. It is little known that lard, for all its reputation, has approximately half the cholesterol of butter.

MANGO: The skin of this oval fruit is washed in gold, pink, red and parrot green. The flesh is deep yellow, juicy and richly perfumed. Mangoes have flat, oval pits. To slice the fruit, free it from the pit in large pieces.

MASA: Literally, "dough" in Spanish. *Masa* is cornmeal dough made from dried corn kernels that have been softened in a lime (calcium hydroxide) solution, then ground. Fresh *masa* is commercially available in Mexico, but it is tricky to work with and dries out quickly. *Masa* comes finely ground, for tortillas, and coarsely ground, for tamales. It is easier to use Instant Corn Flour Tortilla Mix (above) when making tortillas.

PAPAYA: A nearly oval fruit with creamy golden yellow skin, orange-yellow flesh and scores of shiny black seeds conveniently packed in its center. When slightly underripe, the flesh is firm (perfect for making into relishes); when ripe, it is so juicy as to be almost melting.

PEPPER: There is a *Piper nigrum*, peppercorn, and the *Capsicum frutescens* and *Capsicum' annuum*, the families of vegetables known variously as peppers and chiles. Peppercorns came to the Western world originally from Madagascar. The success of medieval spice traders made black pepper more widely available and only a little less precious than it had previously been.

Representing the *frutescens* contingent, bell peppers are related to chiles but lack capsaicin (the compound that makes them hot). Bell peppers are therefore known as "sweet." Until recently, bell peppers of any color other than green were an oddity at many markets; today there is a profusion of yellow, orange, red and purple ones. Red and yellow are acknowledged to be the sweetest. Roast bell peppers as for chiles (page 12).

PINE NUTS: (*piñons, pignolis*): Pine nuts are the seeds of the piñon pine. They are delicious raw or toasted. Store them tightly covered and either refrigerated or frozen, depending on how quickly they are to be used.

RED PEPPER: See Ground Red Pepper

RED PEPPER SAUCE: This commercially bottled condiment is made from vinegar, spices and hot chiles. It adds heat but little in the way of flavor.

RICE: Mexican cooking calls for long-grain or medium-grain white rice.

TEQUILA: A pale, sharp-tasting liquor distilled from the agave plant, which thrives in an arid, hot climate. The stem of the agave, known also as the "century plant," is used in making both *pulque* and tequila.

TOMATILLO: These fat little vegetables are the size of robust cherry tomatoes. They grow in papery husks reminiscent of Japanese lanterns and taste best when they are brilliant green in color. By the time they begin to turn yellow, they have lost some of their acid freshness. This happens when they are lightly cooked too, but then, although they relinquish their vibrant color, they develop a gentler flavor and become more luscious. Uncooked, chopped tomatillos are the basis for chunky green salsas. Select tomatillos with their husks still drawn tightly around them. Husk and rinse off the sticky residue before using them.

TOMATO: Roasting tomatoes gives them a faintly mysterious flavor. It works best with truly ripe, red tomatoes.

To roast and peel tomatoes: Set oven control to broil. Arrange cored tomatoes with their top surfaces about 5 inches from the heat. Broil, turning occasionally, until the skin is blistered and evenly browned, 5 to 8 minutes. The skins will be easy to remove. If the tomatoes are roasted on aluminum foil, clean-up will be easy and you'll be able to save any juice they give off as they roast.

TORTILLA: Tortillas are round, flat unleavened breads made from ground wheat or corn. They are the basis of Mexican cookery. Tortillas are rolled, folded, used as dippers, fried crisp and munched fresh. Corn tortillas are cut into wedges and fried for chips. For the best chips, fry tortillas that are at least one day old. Flour tortillas, softer than those made from corn, are more popular in northern Mexico where corn does not flourish; wheat was brought there by the Spanish. Commercially made tortillas of both kinds are best stored in the freezer until needed.

To soften tortillas, warm them on a hot, ungreased skillet or griddle for about 30 seconds to 1 minute. They can be warmed in a 250° oven for 15 minutes. Or, wrap several in dampened, microwavable paper toweling or microwave plastic wrap and microwave on high (100% power) for 15 to 20 seconds.

Mexican Menus

INFORMAL DINNER
Guacamole with Tortilla Chips (page 1)
Chicken Tostadas (page 31)
Biscochitos and Piñon Candy (page 77)

MEXICAN LUNCHEON
Snappy Stuffed Tomatillos (page 4)
Grilled Shrimp (page 45)
Tossed Green Salad
Corn Bread (page 25)
Mango with Passion Fruit (page 74)

HELP-YOURSELF DINNER
Nachos (page 6)
Fajitas (page 50)
Orange and Jícama Salad (page 13)
Mexican Sundaes (page 80)

SOUTH-OF-THE-BORDER BRUNCH
Chunky Tuna Salsa (page 8) with Cut-up Vegetables
Ranch-style Eggs (page 68)
Rio Grande Melon Salad (page 15)
Brown Sugar Rolls (page 26)
Lemon Fruit Tart (page 79)

SPICY DINNER
Cheese Chiles (page 2)
Arroz con Pollo (page 27)
Colorful Pepper Skillet (page 18)
Easy Mexican Chocolate Torte (page 81)

COMPANY FARE
Bell Pepper Rajas (page 6)
Chicken Cilantro (page 30)
Brown Rice with Almonds
Mexican Succotash (page 15)
Strawberry Margarita Pie (page 81)

1
Appetizers

Guacamole

Great as a dip or served with tacos, burritos or tostados.

2 large ripe avocados, mashed
2 medium tomatoes, finely chopped
(about 1½ cups)
1 medium onion, chopped (about ½ cup)
2 jalapeño chiles, seeded and finely
chopped
1 clove garlic, finely chopped
2 tablespoons finely snipped fresh
cilantro
1 tablespoon vegetable oil
Juice of ½ lime (about 2 tablespoons)
½ teaspoon salt
Dash of pepper

Mix all ingredients in glass or plastic bowl. Cover and refrigerate at least 1 hour. Serve with tortilla chips if desired.   **About 2½ cups dip**

PER TABLESPOON: Calories 25; Protein 0 g; Carbohydrate 2 g; Fat 2 g; Cholesterol 0 mg; Sodium 30 mg

CREAMY GUACAMOLE: Stir ¼ cup mayonnaise or salad dressing into avocado mixture before adding tomatoes.

How to Make Your Own Tortilla Chips

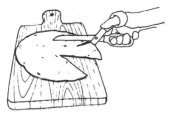

Cut flour or corn tortillas into wedges with kitchen scissors.

Heat vegetable oil (1 inch) to 365°. Fry wedges until crisp and golden brown, about 1 minute.

Drain on paper towels. Sprinkle with salt if desired.

Bean and Garlic Dip

2 cups Pinto Beans (page 20)
¼ cup mayonnaise or salad dressing
1 clove garlic, finely chopped
1½ teaspoons ground red chiles
¼ teaspoon salt
Dash of pepper

Mix all ingredients. Cover and refrigerate 1 hour. Serve with tortilla chips.   **About 2 cups dip**

PER TABLESPOON: Calories 25; Protein 1 g; Carbohydrate 3 g; Fat 1 g; Cholesterol 0 mg; Sodium 30 mg

Mexi-Dip

½ pound ground beef
½ teaspoon dry mustard
¼ to ½ teaspoon chile powder
1 small onion, finely chopped (about ¼ cup)
½ medium green bell pepper, finely chopped (about ¼ cup)
1 can (16 ounces) refried beans
1 can (8 ounces) tomato sauce
1 package (¼ ounces) taco seasoning mix
Sour Cream Topping (right)
Finely shredded lettuce
Shredded Cheddar cheese

Cook ground beef in 10-inch skillet, stirring occasionally, until brown; drain. Stir in mustard, chile powder, onion, bell pepper, beans, tomato sauce and seasoning mix (dry). Heat to boiling, stirring constantly. Spread in ungreased pie plate, 9 × 1¼ inches.

Prepare Sour Cream Topping. Spread topping over ground beef mixture. Sprinkle with lettuce and cheese. Serve with tortilla chips or fresh vegetable slices if desired.

About 3½ cups dip

PER TABLESPOON: Calories 30; Protein 1 g; Carbohydrate 1 g; Fat 2 g; Cholesterol 5 mg; Sodium 40 mg

Sour Cream Topping

1 cup sour cream
2 tablespoons shredded Cheddar cheese
¼ teaspoon chile powder

Mix all ingredients.

MICROWAVE DIRECTIONS: Crumble ground beef into 2-quart microwavable casserole. Cover tightly and microwave on high 2 to 4 minutes, stirring after 2 minutes, until no longer pink; drain. Stir in mustard, chile powder, onion, bell pepper, beans, tomato sauce and seasoning mix (dry). Cover tightly and microwave 4 to 6 minutes, stirring after 2 minutes, until boiling. Continue as directed.

Cheese Chiles

Cheese Chiles can be prepared several days ahead of time; replace the cilantro "stems" before serving.

1 cup shredded Cheddar cheese (4 ounces)
1 cup shredded Colby cheese (4 ounces)
1 teaspoon ground red chiles
1 bunch cilantro stems, cut into ½-inch pieces
Paprika

Place all ingredients except cilantro and paprika in food processor workbowl fitted with steel blade; cover and process until smooth, about 1 minute. Roll mixture by teaspoonfuls into chile shapes.

Insert cilantro pieces in wide ends of shapes for stems. Sprinkle with paprika. Cover and refrigerate until serving time.   **48 appetizers**

PER APPETIZER: Calories 20; Protein 1 g; Carbohydrate 0 g; Fat 2 g; Cholesterol 5 mg; Sodium 30 mg

Cheese Chiles

Spicy Tortilla Chips

These low-calorie chips are very nice served with Green Sauce, page 11.

**2 tablespoons margarine or butter,
  melted**
½ teaspoon chile powder
**8 corn or flour tortillas (8 inches in
  diameter)**

Heat oven to 400°. Mix margarine and chile powder; brush on one side of tortillas. Cut each into 12 wedges. Place on ungreased jelly roll pan, 15½ × 10½ × 1 inch. Bake uncovered 8 to 10 minutes or until crisp and golden brown; cool. (Tortillas will continue to crisp as they cool.) **96 chips**

PER CHIP: Calories 10; Protein 0 g; Carbohydrate 1 g; Fat 0 g; Cholesterol 0 mg; Sodium 3 mg

Snappy Stuffed Tomatillos

Tomatillos grow in papery husks that are easily peeled away, revealing their green, sticky skins.

**20 tomatillos or cherry tomatoes (1¼ to
  1½ inches)**
⅔ cup shredded Cheddar cheese
½ cup whole kernel corn
**2 packages (3 ounces each) cream
  cheese, softened**
2 green onions (with tops), sliced
1 teaspoon ground red chiles
Ground red chiles

Cut thin slice from stem ends of tomatillos. Remove pulp and seeds with melon baller or small spoon.

Mix Cheddar cheese, corn, cream cheese, onions and 1 teaspoon ground red chiles. Fill toma-

tillos with cheese mixture; sprinkle with ground red chiles. Cover and refrigerate until serving time. **20 appetizers**

PER APPETIZER: Calories 50; Protein 2 g; Carbohydrate 4 g; Fat 15 g; Cholesterol 15 mg; Sodium 65 mg

Mexican Deviled Eggs

A nice twist on standard deviled eggs!

12 hard-cooked eggs
¼ cup mayonnaise or salad dressing
**1 jalapeño pepper, seeded and finely
  chopped**
1 tablespoon ground cumin
1 tablespoon finely chopped capers
1 tablespoon prepared mustard
½ teaspoon salt
Chile powder
Finely snipped cilantro leaves

Cut peeled eggs lengthwise into halves. Slip out yolks; mash with fork. Stir in mayonnaise, pepper, cumin, capers, mustard and salt; mix until smooth.

Fill egg whites with egg yolk mixture, heaping lightly. Sprinkle with chile powder; garnish with cilantro. **2 dozen appetizers**

PER APPETIZER: Calories 60; Protein 3 g; Carbohydrate 1 g; Fat 5 g; Cholesterol 110 mg; Sodium 100 mg

Spicy Tortilla Chips with Green Sauce (page 11)

Nachos

The "original" nachos—super simple chips with broiled cheese on top.

Vegetable oil
6 flour or corn tortillas
1½ cups shredded cheese (6 ounces)
6 jalapeño chiles

Heat oil (1 inch) in arge skillet to 365°. Fry tortillas, one at a time, holding tortilla down in oil with tongs, until light brown, about 1 minute; drain.

Place tortillas on ungreased cookie sheet. Sprinkle ¼ cup cheese evenly over each tortilla. Seed and cut each jalapeño chile into 6 strips; arrange strips on top of cheese. Set oven control to broil. Broil tortillas with tops 3 to 4 inches from heat until cheese is melted. Cut each tortilla into 6 wedges.   **36 appetizers**

PER SERVING: Calories 55; Protein 2 g; Carbohydrate 5 g; Fat 3 g; Cholesterol 5 mg; Sodium 55 mg

Chile con Queso Dip

1 cup shredded Cheddar or Monterey
   Jack cheese (4 ounces)
1 can (4 ounces) chopped green chiles,
   drained
¼ cup half-and-half
2 tablespoons finely chopped onion
2 teaspoons ground cumin
½ teaspoon salt

Heat all ingredients over low heat, stirring constantly, until cheese is melted. Serve warm with tortilla chips.   **1¼ cups dip**

PER SERVING: Calories 30; Protein 2 g; Carbohydrate 1 g; Fat 2 g; Cholesterol 5 mg; Sodium 160 mg

Bell Pepper Rajas

Rajas ("strips") usually refers to ribbons of chiles. To prepare rajas *in the microwave oven, arrange strips on a microwave-safe serving plate. Sprinkle with toppings and cover loosely with waxed paper. Microwave on high 1 minute; rotate plate one quarter turn. Microwave 30 to 60 seconds longer, until the cheese has melted.*

½ green bell pepper, seeded and cut into
   6 strips
½ red bell pepper, seeded and cut into
   6 strips
½ yellow bell pepper, seeded and cut
   into 6 strips
¾ cup shredded Monterey Jack cheese
   (3 ounces)
2 tablespoons chopped ripe olives
¼ teaspoon crushed red pepper

Cut bell pepper strips crosswise into halves. Arrange in ungreased broilerproof pie pan, 9 × 1¼ inches, or round pan, 9 × 2 inches. Sprinkle with cheese, olives and red pepper.

Set oven control to broil. Broil peppers with tops 3 to 4 inches from heat until cheese is melted, about 3 minutes.   **6 servings**

PER SERVING: Calories 65; Protein 3 g; Carbohydrate 2 g; Fat 5 g; Cholesterol 15 mg; Sodium 115 mg

Bell Pepper Rajas

Chunky Tuna Salsa

Here is a wonderful new use for that Mexican staple, salsa.

1 can (6½ ounces) tuna, well drained
¾ cup chopped red onion (about 1 large)
1 large tomato, chopped
1 jalapeño pepper, seeded and chopped
1 tablespoon lemon juice
Snipped fresh cilantro leaves

Break up tuna with fork. Gently mix tuna and remaining ingredients except cilantro and tortilla chips. Sprinkle with cilantro. Serve with tortilla chips.   **About 2½ cups salsa**

PER TABLESPOON: Calories 8; Protein 1 g; Carbohydrate 1 g; Fat 0 g; Cholesterol 0 mg; Sodium 15 mg

Peanuts in Chile

2 cloves garlic, crushed
1 teaspoon vegetable oil
1 cup shelled raw peanuts
1 tablespoon chile powder
½ teaspoon salt

Cook and stir garlic in oil in 8-inch skillet over medium heat until golden brown; remove garlic. Add peanuts and chile powder. Cook and stir until peanuts are warm, about 2 minutes. Drain on paper towels; sprinkle with salt.

1 cup peanuts

PER CUP: Calories 255; Protein 10 g; Carbohydrate 9 g; Fat 20 g; Cholesterol 0 mg; Sodium 290 mg

Tortilla Wedges

½ cup Fresh Tomato Salsa (page 11) or prepared salsa
½ cup sour cream or plain yogurt
¼ cup chopped red bell pepper
½ cup finely chopped cooked chicken
8 flour tortillas (about 8 inches in diameter)
¼ cup Guacamole (page 1) or frozen (thawed) guacamole
½ cup Refried Beans (page 20)
1 cup shredded Cheddar or Monterey Jack cheese (4 ounces)

Heat oven to 350°. Prepare Fresh Tomato Salsa and mix with sour cream. Reserve half of the salsa mixture. Mix the remaining salsa mixture, half of the bell pepper and the chicken. Place 2 tortillas on ungreased cookie sheet and spread with chicken mixture. Prepare Guacamole. Spread 2 tortillas with Guacamole and place on chicken mixture. Spread 2 more tortillas with refried beans and place on Guacamole. Top each stack with remaining salsa, a tortilla, bell pepper and cheese.

Bake about 15 minutes or until cheese is melted and filling is hot. Cut each stack into 8 wedges.   **16 appetizers**

PER SERVING: Calories 95; Protein 4 g; Carbohydrate 8 g; Fat 6 g; Cholesterol 15 mg; Sodium 180 mg

Mexican Cheese Puffs

1 cup Bisquick® original baking mix
3 tablespoons margarine or butter,
    softened
1 egg
3 tablespoons chopped green chiles
1 cup shredded Cheddar cheese (about
    4 ounces)

Heat oven to 400°. Mix Bisquick® baking mix, margarine, egg and chiles; stir in cheese. Drop dough by rounded teaspoonfuls about 1 inch apart onto greased cookie sheet. Bake until golden brown, 10 to 12 minutes.

About 2 dozen appetizers

PER SERVING: Calories 55; Protein 2 g; Carbohydrate 3 g; Fat 4 g; Cholesterol 15 mg; Sodium 120 mg

SAUSAGE CHEESE PUFFS: Substitute ¼ cup finely crumbled uncooked bulk pork sausage for the margarine. Bake 12 to 15 minutes.

DO-AHEAD TIP: Dough can be placed in bowl or spooned onto cookie sheet, covered and refrigerated no longer than 24 hours.

Mexican Rice Morsels

Great for parties.

2 cups cooked brown or regular long
    grain rice
½ cup all-purpose flour
½ teaspoon salt
¼ teaspoon pepper
2 eggs, beaten
2 ounces Monterey Jack cheese with jala-
    peño chiles
¾ cup crushed tortilla chips (about
    3 cups)
Vegetable oil

Mix rice, flour, salt, pepper and eggs. Cut cheese into twenty-four ½-inch cubes. With wet hands, shape about 1 tablespoon rice mixture around each cheese cube. Roll rice balls in tortilla chips.

Heat oil (2 to 3 inches) in deep fryer or Dutch oven to 375°. Fry rice morsels 4 to 6 at a time 3 to 3½ minutes or until golden brown. Remove with slotted spoon. Drain on paper towels; keep warm. Repeat with remaining rice balls. Serve with salsa, guacamole and sour cream if desired.

2 dozen appetizers

PER SERVING: Calories 85; Protein 2 g; Carbohydrate 9 g; Fat 5 g; Cholesterol 25 mg; Sodium 160 mg

Empanaditas

Empanaditas *("little* empanadas*") are baked or fried pastries stuffed with savory or sweet fillings.*

½ **pound ground beef**
1 **small onion, finely chopped (about**
  ¼ **cup)**
2 **tablespoons raisins, chopped**
2 **tablespoons chopped green olives**
¼ **teaspoon salt**
⅛ **teaspoon pepper**
¼ **cup small curd creamed cottage**
  cheese
1 **hard-cooked egg, peeled and chopped**
1 **egg, separated**
1 **teaspoon water**
Pastry dough for 10-inch 2-crust pie
2 **teaspoons milk**

Cook and stir ground beef in 10-inch skillet, breaking up into small pieces, until brown; drain, reserving 1 tablespoon fat and the beef in skillet. Stir in onion, raisins, olives, salt and pepper. Cover and cook over low heat 5 minutes. Stir in cottage cheese and hard-cooked egg.

Heat oven to 400°. Mix egg white and water until slightly foamy; reserve. Prepare pastry dough; gather into a ball. Divide into halves. Shape into 2 flattened rounds on lightly floured cloth-covered surface. Roll 1 round of pastry into circle, about 14 inches in diameter. Cut into 11 or 12 circles, 3½ inches in diameter.

Spoon 2 teaspoons beef mixture onto center of each circle; brush edge of pastry with egg white mixture. Fold pastry circle up over filling; press edge with fork to seal. Place empanaditas on ungreased cookie sheet. Repeat with remaining round of pastry and filling. Gather any remaining pastry; shape into another round. Repeat rolling, cutting and filling.

Beat egg yolk and milk until well blended; brush over tops of empanaditas. Bake until golden brown, 15 to 20 minutes. Serve warm.

About 34 empanaditas

PER SERVING: Calories 105; Protein 3 g; Carbohydrate 8 g; Fat 7 g; Cholesterol 15 mg; Sodium 105 mg

2

Sizzling Sauces and Sides

Fresh Tomato Salsa

Here is the all-purpose Mexican favorite. If time permits, refrigerate the salsa for two or three hours before serving, so that the flavors of individual ingredients "marry." Serve this with tortilla dishes, grilled chicken or hamburger, or tortilla chips.

3 medium tomatoes, seeded and
   chopped (about 3 cups)
1/2 cup sliced green onions (with tops)
1/2 cup chopped green bell pepper (about
   1 medium)
2 to 3 tablespoons lime juice
2 tablespoons snipped fresh cilantro
1 tablespoon finely chopped jalapeño
   chile
1 teaspoon finely chopped garlic (about
   3 cloves)
1/2 teaspoon salt

Mix all ingredients.   **About 3 1/2 cups salsa**

PER TABLESPOON: Calories 4; Protein 0 g; Carbohydrate 1 g; Fat 0 g; Cholesterol 0 mg; Sodium 20 mg

Green Sauce

This is a suave chile sauce, slightly chunky and rich with cream.

1 large onion, finely chopped (about
   1 cup)
4 poblano chiles, roasted, peeled (right),
   seeded and finely chopped (about
   1/2 cup)
1 jalapeño chile, seeded and finely
   chopped
1 clove garlic, finely chopped
2 tablespoons vegetable oil
1/2 cup whipping (heavy) cream
1/4 teaspoon salt

Cook onion, chiles and garlic in oil over medium heat, stirring occasionally, until onion is tender, about 8 minutes. Stir in whipping cream and salt.   **About 1 1/3 cups sauce**

PER TABLESPOON: Calories 30; Protein 0 g; Carbohydrate 1 g; Fat 3 g; Cholesterol 5 mg; Sodium 30 mg

Roasting Chiles

Recipes often call for chiles to be roasted. This enhances the flavor and makes them a snap to peel. Roasted chiles may be frozen before peeling, a convenience if you roast a big batch at once; wrap them airtight in plastic wrap.

Broiler Method

Set oven control to broil. Arrange whole chiles with their top surfaces about 5 inches from the heat. (Some people cut a small slit in the shoulder of each chile, to prevent it from bursting.) Broil, turning occasionally, until the skin is blistered and evenly browned (*not* burned). Remove chiles to a plastic bag and close tightly; let chiles sit for 20 minutes, then peel. Anaheim and poblano chiles will roast in 12 to 17 minutes; jalapeño and serrano chiles, in about 5 minutes.

Basic Red Sauce

This smooth sauce has a gentle ancho flavor. It is a superb all-around tomato sauce, perfect for serving with tacos and enchiladas.

- 8 ancho chiles
- 3½ cups warm water
- 1 medium onion, chopped (about ½ cup)
- 2 cloves garlic, chopped
- ¼ cup vegetable oil
- 1 can (8 ounces) tomato sauce
- 1 tablespoon dried oregano leaves
- 1 tablespoon cumin seed
- 1 teaspoon salt

Cover chiles with warm water. Let stand until softened, about 30 minutes; drain. Strain liquid; reserve. Remove stems, seeds and membranes from chiles.

Cook and stir onion and garlic in oil in 2-quart saucepan until onion is tender. Stir in chiles, 2 cups of the reserved liquid and the remaining ingredients. Heat to boiling; reduce heat. Simmer uncovered 20 minutes; cool.

Pour into food processor workbowl fitted with steel blade or into blender container; cover and process until smooth. Cover and refrigerate up to 10 days. **About 2½ cups sauce**

PER TABLESPOON: Calories 18; Protein 0 g; Carbohydrate 2 g; Fat 1 g; Cholesterol 0 mg; Sodium 90 mg

Black Bean Relish

This is a dramatic relish: dark, with bright red pieces of bell pepper and tomato. Serve it with tortillas, salads and simple grilled chicken or poached fish.

- 1 can (15 ounces) black beans, rinsed and drained
- 1 medium tomato, finely chopped (about ¾ cup)
- 1 serrano chile, seeded and finely chopped
- ½ cup chopped red bell pepper (about 1 medium)
- ¼ cup finely chopped red onion (about 1 small)
- 2 tablespoons white wine vinegar
- 1 tablespoon vegetable oil
- ¼ teaspoon salt

Mix all ingredients. Cover and refrigerate until chilled, about 1 hour. **2½ cups relish**

PER TABLESPOON: Calories 16; Protein 1 g; Carbohydrate 3 g; Fat 0 g; Cholesterol 0 mg; Sodium 40 mg

Orange and Jícama Salad

The Southwest loves its oranges and jícama, and this salad from Mexico adds sweet red onion to that crisp-juicy combination. If you like, substitute 2 apples cut into thin wedges for the jícama.

3 tablespoons vegetable oil
2 tablespoons vinegar
½ teaspoon salt
3 medium oranges, pared and sectioned
1 small red onion, thinly sliced and separated into rings
1 medium green, red or yellow bell pepper, cut into 1-inch pieces
8 ounces jícama, pared and cut into 1½ × ½-inch strips
Chile powder or paprika

Mix oil, vinegar and salt in large bowl. Add remaining ingredients except chile powder; toss. Sprinkle lightly with chile powder. Serve on lettuce leaves if desired. **6 servings**

PER SERVING: Calories 120; Protein 1 g; Carbohydrate 13 g; Fat 7 g; Cholesterol 0 mg; Sodium 180 mg

Christmas Eve Salad

Christmas is a high celebration in Mexico. This festive, brilliantly colored salad is an example of that exuberance. The vegetables take on a rosy hue, thanks to the beet juice.

2 medium oranges, pared and sectioned
2 medium bananas, sliced
1 can (8¼ ounces) sliced beets, drained (reserve liquid)
1 can (8 ounces) pineapple chunks in juice, drained (reserve juice)
½ jícama, pared and sliced, or 1 can (8 ounces) water chestnuts, drained and sliced
2 tablespoons lemon juice
2 tablespoons sugar
½ teaspoon salt
3 cups shredded lettuce
1 lime, cut into wedges
¼ cup chopped peanuts
⅓ cup pomegranate seeds or sliced radishes
1 tablespoon anise seed
1 tablespoon sugar

Place oranges, bananas, beets, pineapple and jícama in bowl. Mix reserved beet liquid, pineapple juice, the lemon juice, 2 tablespoons sugar and the salt; pour over fruit. Let stand 10 minutes; drain.

Arrange fruit on shredded lettuce. Garnish with lime, peanuts and pomegranate seeds. Mix anise seed and 1 tablespoon sugar; sprinkle over salad. **8 servings**

PER SERVING: Calories 150; Protein 3 g; Carbohydrate 28 g; Fat 3 g; Cholesterol 0 mg; Sodium 200 mg

Rio Grande Melon Salad

Rio Grande Melon Salad

2 cups watermelon balls
2 mangoes or papayas, pared and sliced
½ honeydew melon, pared, seeded and
  thinly sliced
¾ cup seedless red grape halves
1 large bunch watercress
Honey-Lime Dressing (below)

Prepare Honey-Lime Dressing. Arrange fruits on watercress. Drizzle with Honey-Lime Dressing.

6 servings

PER SERVING: Calories 250; Protein 1 g; Carbohydrate 32 g; Fat 13 g; Cholesterol 0 mg; Sodium 20 mg

Honey-Lime Dressing

⅓ cup vegetable oil
¼ teaspoon grated lime peel
2 tablespoons lime juice
1 tablespoon honey

Shake all ingredients in tightly covered container.

Mexican Succotash

A tasty vegetable medley.

3 medium zucchini
2 ears fresh corn
1 medium onion, chopped (about ½ cup)
¼ cup vegetable oil
1 can (28 ounces) Italian plum tomatoes
1 teaspoon dried oregano leaves
½ teaspoon salt
Dash of pepper

Cut zucchini into ½-inch slices. Cut kernels from corn. Cook and stir onion in oil in 10-inch skillet over medium heat until tender. Add zucchini; cook and stir 1 minute. Stir in corn and re-maining ingredients. Heat to boiling; reduce heat. Cover and simmer until zucchini is tender, about 15 minutes.

6 servings

PER SERVING: Calories 165; Protein 3 g; Carbohydrate 16 g; Fat 10 g; Cholesterol 0 mg; Sodium 400 mg

NOTE: 1 package (10 ounces) frozen corn can be substituted for the fresh corn.

Mexican Corn Pudding

Made with evaporated milk and eggs, this pudding is rich. It doesn't feature any of the strong spices associated with Mexican food, so as a side dish it would be appropriate with just about any noncreamy main dish. Raisins and vanilla extract add a gentle sweetness.

1 can (12 ounces) evaporated milk
¼ cup all-purpose flour
2 cans (about 16 ounces each) cream-
  style corn
4 eggs, slightly beaten
½ cup sugar
¼ cup raisins
1 teaspoon baking soda
1 teaspoon salt
1 teaspoon vanilla

Shake ½ cup of the milk and the flour in tightly covered container. Mix milk mixture, remaining milk and the remaining ingredients. Pour into greased square pan, 9 × 9 × 2 inches. Bake uncovered in 350° oven until knife inserted halfway between center and edge comes out clean, about 1 hour.

8 servings

PER SERVING: Calories 275; Protein 10 g; Carbohydrate 45 g; Fat 6 g; Cholesterol 115 mg; Sodium 820 mg

Black Bean Salad

Black Bean Salad

Chile Dressing (below)
1 cup frozen whole kernel corn, rinsed to
thaw and drained
1 cup diced jícama (about 5 ounces)
1 medium tomato, seeded and chopped
(about ¾ cup)
2 cans (15 ounces each) black beans,
rinsed and drained
2 green onions (with tops), sliced

Prepare Chile Dressing in large glass or plastic
bowl. Stir in remaining ingredients.

PER SERVING: Calories 440; Protein 21 g; Carbohydrate 71 g; Fat 8 g; Cholesterol 0 mg; Sodium 520 mg

Chile Dressing

¼ cup red wine vinegar
2 tablespoons vegetable oil
½ teaspoon chile powder
¼ teaspoon ground cumin
1 small clove garlic, crushed

Mix all ingredients.

Cauliflower Wedges with Salsa

1 medium head cauliflower (about
2 pounds)
2½ cups chopped seeded tomatoes
(about 3 medium)
½ cup chopped onion (about 1 medium)
1 can (4 ounces) chopped green chiles,
drained
½ teaspoon salt
¼ teaspoon ground cinnamon
2 tablespoons chopped ripe olives

Heat 1 inch water to boiling. Add cauliflower.
Cover and heat to boiling; reduce heat. Simmer
until tender, 20 to 25 minutes; drain. Cook and
stir remaining ingredients except olives in 10-
inch nonstick skillet over medium heat until hot.
Place cauliflower on serving plate. Cut into 8
wedges; separate wedges slightly. Spoon tomato mixture over and around cauliflower
wedges. Sprinkle with olives.   **8 servings**

PER SERVING: Calories 35; Protein 1 g; Carbohydrate 6 g; Fat 1 g; Cholesterol 0 mg; Sodium 165 mg

MICROWAVE DIRECTIONS: Cut cone-shaped center
from core of cauliflower. Place cauliflower and
¼ cup water in microwavable pie plate, 9 × 1¼
inches. Cover tightly and microwave on high 4
minutes; rotate pie plate ½ turn. Microwave until
tender, 3 to 4 minutes longer; drain. Mix remaining ingredients except olives in microwavable 1½-quart casserole. Microwave uncovered
until hot, 4 to 7 minutes. Continue as directed.

NOTE: Tomatoes vary in moisture. If necessary,
spoon off extra liquid before topping cauliflower.

Colorful Pepper Skillet

This dish is simply beautiful. Four brightly colored peppers, shiny with a touch of oil, are seasoned with cumin seed and the fresh flavor of cilantro.

1 teaspoon olive or vegetable oil
4 small bell peppers (green, purple, red and yellow), cut into strips
1 medium onion, thinly sliced
2 cloves garlic, finely chopped
1 tablespoon snipped fresh
    or 1 teaspoon dried cilantro leaves
1 teaspoon cumin seed

Heat oil in 10-inch nonstick skillet over medium-high heat until hot. Stir in remaining ingredients. Cook, stirring occasionally, until peppers are crisp-tender, 4 to 5 minutes.   **6 servings**

PER SERVING: Calories 40; Protein 1 g; Carbohydrate 7 g; Fat 1 g; Cholesterol 0 mg; Sodium 200 mg

Stewed Mexican Vegetables

1 medium onion, chopped (about ½ cup)
2 tablespoons margarine or butter
2 tablespoons vegetable oil
1 medium zucchini, chopped
4 tomatoes, chopped
¼ cup snipped fresh parsley
2 tablespoons chile powder
¼ teaspoon ground nutmeg
¼ teaspoon ground cinnamon
Corn Batter (right)

Prepare Corn Batter. Cook and stir onion in margarine and oil in 10-inch skillet until tender. Stir in remaining ingredients except Corn Batter. Heat to boiling; reduce heat. Simmer uncovered 10 minutes. Prepare Corn Batter; drop by rounded teaspoonfuls onto hot sauce. Cook uncovered over low heat 10 minutes. Cover and cook 10 minutes longer.   **10 servings**

PER SERVING: Calories 150; Protein 5 g; Carbohydrate 15 g; Fat 8 g; Cholesterol 30 mg; Sodium 250 mg

Corn Batter

1 can (8¾ ounces) whole kernel corn, drained
¼ cup milk
¼ cup chopped pimiento
¼ teaspoon salt
Dash of pepper
½ cup all-purpose flour
½ cup shredded cheese (about 2 ounces)
½ teaspoon baking powder
1 egg, separated

Mix all ingredients except egg white. Beat egg white in small mixer bowl until stiff but not dry. Fold corn mixture into egg white.

Cinnamon Squash Rings

2 tablespoons packed brown sugar
2 tablespoons milk
1 egg
¾ cup soft bread crumbs (about 2½ slices bread)
¼ cup yellow or white cornmeal
2 teaspoons ground cinnamon
1 large acorn squash (about 1½ pounds), cut crosswise into ½-inch slices and seeded
⅓ cup margarine or butter, melted

Heat oven to 400°. Mix brown sugar, milk and egg. Mix bread crumbs, cornmeal and cinnamon. Dip squash slices into egg mixture and coat with bread crumb mixture; repeat.

Place in ungreased rectangular pan, 13 × 9 × 2 inches; drizzle with margarine. Bake uncovered until squash is tender, 30 to 35 minutes.
                                6 servings

PER SERVING: Calories 225; Protein 4 g; Carbohydrate 25 g; Fat 12 g; Cholesterol 35 mg; Sodium 220 mg

Cinnamon Squash Rings

Pinto Beans

Pinto beans are a staple of Mexican cooking.

4 cups water
1 pound dried pinto or black beans
   (about 2 cups)
1 medium onion, chopped (about ½ cup)
¼ cup vegetable oil
2 cloves garlic, crushed
1 slice bacon
1 teaspoon salt
1 teaspoon cumin seed

Mix water, beans and onion in 4-quart Dutch oven. Cover and heat to boiling; boil 2 minutes. Remove from heat; let stand 1 hour.

Add just enough water to beans to cover. Stir in remaining ingredients. Heat to boiling; reduce heat. Cover and boil gently, stirring occasionally, until beans are very tender, about 2 hours. (Add water during cooking if necessary.) Drain; reserve broth for recipes calling for bean broth. Cover and refrigerate beans and broth separately; use within 10 days.   **8 servings**

PER SERVING: Calories 270; Protein 12 g; Carbohydrate 37 g; Fat 8 g; Cholesterol 1 mg; Sodium 280 mg

NOTE: Canned pinto beans can be substituted in recipes calling for Pinto Beans. One can (15 ounces) pinto beans, drained, yields about 2 cups.

Frontier Beans

Hearty beans for big appetites.

1 cup sliced green onions (with tops)
½ pound chorizo sausage links, chopped
2 cans (16 ounces each) pinto beans, 1
   can drained
3 small poblano chiles, roasted, peeled,
   seeded and chopped
1 large tomato, chopped (about 1 cup)
¼ teaspoon salt

Heat oven to 350°. Cook and stir onions and sausage until sausage is done; drain.

Mix sausage mixture and remaining ingredients in ungreased 2-quart casserole. Bake uncovered until hot and bubbly, about 30 minutes.

6 servings

PER SERVING: Calories 390; Protein 22 g; Carbohydrate 42 g; Fat 15 g; Cholesterol 35 mg; Sodium 900 mg

Refried Beans

½ cup vegetable oil or lard
2 cups cooked Pinto Beans (left)
2 tablespoons chile powder
1 tablespoon ground cumin
1 teaspoon salt
⅛ teaspoon pepper

Heat lard in 10-inch skillet over medium heat until hot. Add Pinto Beans; cook, stirring occasionally, 5 minutes. Mash beans; stir in chile powder, cumin, salt and pepper. Add more oil to skillet if necessary; cook and stir until a smooth paste forms, about 5 minutes. Garnish with shredded cheese if desired.   **4 servings**

PER SERVING: Calories 395; Protein 8 g; Carbohydrate 25 g; Fat 29 g; Cholesterol 0 mg; Sodium 580 mg

NOTE: Canned refried beans can be substituted in recipes calling for Refried Beans. 1 can (17 ounces) refried beans yields about 2 cups.

Frontier Beans

Mexican Black Beans

2¼ cups water
¾ cup dried black beans
1 tablespoon snipped fresh parsley
1 tablespoon white wine vinegar
1 teaspoon shredded lime or lemon peel
¼ teaspoon red pepper sauce
2 green onions (with tops), thinly sliced
1 medium red or green bell pepper,
    chopped (about 1 cup)

Heat water and beans to boiling in 2-quart saucepan. Boil uncovered 2 minutes; reduce heat. Cover and simmer about 1 hour, stirring occasionally, until beans are tender (do not boil or beans will burst); drain. Stir in remaining ingredients. Cook and stir until mixture is hot.

4 servings

PER SERVING: Calories 135; Protein 8 g; Carbohydrate 25 g; Fat 1 g; Cholesterol 0 mg; Sodium 10 mg

---

About Beans

Beans are an accompaniment to every meal, including breakfast, in many Mexican homes. Usually prepared in large quantities, beans are served the first day with their broth, often with an onion and cilantro garnish. As beans are reheated, the broth thickens and the beans develop a paste-like texture. They are then mashed and fried in lard or oil and become the famous Mexican "refried" beans.

All dried beans are high in vegetable protein, which is fortified when combined with that in meats and dairy products. Store dried beans tightly covered in a dry place 6 to 8 months.

NOTE: Two cans (15 ounces each) black beans, rinsed and drained, can be substituted for the cooked dried black beans.

Refried Bean Bake

Super simple to assemble!

1 can (16 ounces) refried beans or Refried Beans (page 20)
1 medium onion, finely chopped (about ½ cup)
1 small green bell pepper, finely chopped (about ½ cup)
4 eggs
1½ cups shredded Cheddar cheese (6 ounces)
1 teaspoon chile powder
⅛ teaspoon garlic powder
1 jar (12 ounces) salsa or Fresh Tomato Salsa (page 11)

Mix beans, onion, bell pepper, eggs, ¾ cup of the cheese, the chile powder and garlic powder. Pour into ungreased square pan, 9 × 9 × 2 inches; sprinkle with remaining cheese. Bake uncovered in 350° oven until hot and firm, about 30 minutes. Heat salsa, stirring occasionally, until hot; serve with beans.   **8 servings**

PER SERVING: Calories 210; Protein 13 g; Carbohydrate 17 g; Fat 10 g; Cholesterol 130 mg; Sodium 860 mg

Black Bean Soup

1 large onion, chopped (about 1 cup)
4 cloves garlic, finely chopped
2 tablespoons vegetable oil
1 pound dried black beans
2 cups cubed fully cooked smoked ham
6 cups chicken broth
2 tablespoons ground red chiles
2 tablespoons snipped fresh cilantro
  leaves
1 tablespoon dried oregano leaves
2 teaspoons ground cumin
1 can (28 ounces) whole tomatoes,
  undrained
1 canned chipotle chile in adobo sauce
Quick Crème Fraîche (below)
Chopped red bell pepper

Cook and stir onion and garlic in oil in 4-quart Dutch oven until onion is tender. Stir in remaining ingredients except Quick Crème Fraîche and bell pepper; heat to boiling. Boil 2 minutes; reduce heat. Cover and simmer until beans are tender, about 2¼ hours.

Pour ¼ of the soup into food processor workbowl fitted with steel blade or into blender container; cover and process until smooth. Repeat with remaining soup. Serve with Quick Crème Fraîche and bell pepper.   **8 servings**

PER SERVING: Calories 430; Protein 26 g; Carbohydrate 46 g; Fat 16 g; Cholesterol 45 mg; Sodium 1350 mg

Quick Crème Fraîche

⅓ cup whipping (heavy) cream
⅔ cup sour cream

Gradually stir whipping cream into sour cream. Cover and refrigerate up to 48 hours.

Beans and Rice

To serve this as a main dish, increase the serving size to 1 cup.

2 cups water
⅔ cup dried kidney beans (about
  6 ounces)
1 slice bacon, cut up
1 cup chopped green bell pepper (about
  1 medium)
½ cup chopped onion (about 1 medium)
⅔ cup uncooked regular rice
1 teaspoon salt

Heat water and beans to boiling in 3-quart nonstick saucepan. Boil 2 minutes; remove from heat. Cover and let stand 1 hour.

Add enough water to beans to cover if necessary. Heat to boiling; reduce heat. Cover and simmer until tender, 1 to 1½ hours (do not boil or beans will burst).

Drain beans, reserving liquid. Cook bacon in 10-inch skillet until crisp; add bell pepper and onion. Cook and stir until onion is tender. Add enough water to bean liquid to measure 1⅓ cups. Add bean liquid and remaining ingredients to beans in 3-quart saucepan. Heat to boiling, stirring once or twice; reduce heat. Cover and simmer 15 minutes (do not lift cover or stir). Remove from heat. Fluff with fork; cover and let steam 5 to 10 minutes.   **8 servings**

PER SERVING: Calories 70; Protein 3 g; Carbohydrate 10 g; Fat 2 g; Cholesterol 2 mg; Sodium 280 mg

Flour Tortillas

2 cups all-purpose flour
1 teaspoon salt
3 tablespoons shortening or lard
½ cup warm water

Cut lard into flour and salt until particles are size of small peas. Sprinkle in water, 1 tablespoon at a time, until all flour is moistened and dough almost cleans side of bowl. Gather dough into a ball; divide into 12 equal parts. Shape into balls; brush with lard. Cover and let rest 20 minutes.

Roll each ball on floured surface into 6-inch circle. Heat ungreased 8-inch skillet or griddle over medium-high heat until hot. Cook tortilla until dry around edge and blisters appear on surface, about 2 minutes. Turn and cook other side until dry, about 1 minute. Stack tortillas, placing waxed paper between each. Cover with a damp towel. **12 tortillas**

PER SERVING: Calories 100; Protein 2 g; Carbohydrate 16 g; Fat 3 g; Cholesterol 0 mg; Sodium 180 mg

NOTE: Purchased prepared 6-inch flour tortillas can be substituted in recipes calling for Flour Tortillas. Follow package directions for using tortillas.

Corn Tortillas

Masa harina is instant corn flour used in Mexican cooking. It can be found in the specialty food section of some supermarkets, or at Mexican specialty food stores.

Mix 2 cups masa harina and 1¼ cups warm water with hands until all masa harina is moistened and cleans side of bowl. (1 to 2 teaspoons water can be added if necessary.) Cover with damp towel; let rest 10 minutes. Divide into twelve 1-inch balls.

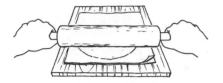

(1) Place each ball on waxed paper square; flatten slightly. Cover with second waxed paper square. Roll into 6-inch circle.

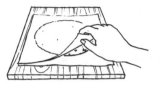

(2) Peel off top square of waxed paper. Heat ungreased 10-inch skillet or griddle over medium-high heat until hot.

(3) Place each tortilla in skillet, waxed paper side up; let cook about 30 seconds. Carefully remove waxed paper square. Cook tortilla until dry around edge, about 1 minute. Turn and cook other side until dry, about 2 minutes. Stack tortillas, placing waxed paper between each. Cover with a damp towel. **12 tortillas**

PER SERVING: Calories 65; Protein 1 g; Carbohydrate 15 g; Fat 0 g; Cholesterol 0 mg; Sodium 0 mg

NOTE: Purchased prepared 6-inch corn tortillas can be substituted in recipes calling for Corn Tortillas. Follow package directions for using tortillas.

About Tortillas

The tortilla is the basic bread of Mexico and is made from flour or corn. Tortillas are good eaten warm and spread with butter. They can be cut into strips, fried and used in main dishes or soups. They are often cut into wedges, fried until crisp and served with dips.

In Mexico, *tacos* are always made with soft tortillas; the crisp tortilla shell is the American version. *Enchiladas* are rolled, filled tortillas covered with a sauce and heated in the oven. *Burritos* are always made with flour tortillas rather than corn tortillas. They can also be fried until crisp, but this is more popular in California and the southwestern United States than in Mexico. *Tostadas* are to Mexican cuisine what hamburgers are to that of the United States. Every region of Mexico has its variation of this open-faced "sandwich."

Corn Bread

1½ cups cornmeal
½ cup all-purpose flour*
¼ cup vegetable oil or shortening
1½ cups buttermilk
2 teaspoons baking powder
1 teaspoon sugar
1 teaspoon salt
½ teaspoon baking soda
2 eggs

Heat oven to 450°. Grease round pan, 9 × 1½ inches, square pan, 8 × 8 × 2 inches, or 10-inch ovenproof skillet. Mix all ingredients. Beat

vigorously 30 seconds. Pour into pan. Bake round or square pan 25 to 30 minutes, skillet about 20 minutes or until golden brown. Serve warm. **12 pieces**

PER SERVING: Calories 100; Protein 3 g; Carbohydrate 9 g; Fat 6 g; Cholesterol 45 mg; Sodium 370 mg

MICROWAVE DIRECTIONS: Mix 2 tablespoons cornmeal and ½ teaspoon paprika. Grease 8-cup microwavable ring dish. Sprinkle evenly with cornmeal mixture. Prepare batter as directed. Pour into dish. Elevate dish on inverted microwavable dinner plate in microwave oven. Microwave uncovered on medium (50%) 11 to 14 minutes, rotating dish ½ turn after 8 minutes, until wooden pick inserted in center comes out clean. (Parts of surface may appear moist but will continue to cook while standing.) Let stand on flat, heatproof surface (not wire rack) 5 minutes. Invert on heatproof serving plate.

CORN MUFFINS: Grease bottoms only of 14 medium muffin cups, 2½ × 1¼ inches. Fill cups about ⅞ full. Bake about 20 minutes. **14 muffins**

MEXICAN DOUBLE CORN BREAD: Decrease buttermilk to 1 cup. Stir in 1 can (8 ounces) cream-style corn, 1 can (4 ounces) chopped green chiles, well drained, and 1 teaspoon chile powder.

*If using self-rising flour, decrease baking powder to 1 teaspoon and omit salt.

Brown Sugar Rolls

The Mexican name for these rolls, chorreadas, means "dirty faces," referring to the dark smudge of Brown Sugar Glaze.

½ **cup packed dark brown sugar**
⅓ **cup vegetable shortening**
2 **teaspoons salt**
1¾ **cups hot water**
1 **package active dry yeast**
Dash of granulated or dark brown sugar
¼ **cup warm water (105 to 115°)**
2 **cups whole wheat flour**
3¾ **to 4 cups all-purpose flour**
1 **egg, slightly beaten**
Brown Sugar Glaze (right)

Place brown sugar, lard and salt in large bowl. Stir in 1¾ cups hot water until brown sugar is dissolved. Dissolve yeast and granulated sugar in ¼ cup warm water; stir into brown sugar mixture. Beat in whole wheat flour and enough all-purpose flour to make dough stiff enough to knead. Turn dough onto lightly floured surface; knead until smooth and elastic, about 10 minutes. Place in greased bowl; turn greased side up. Cover; let rise in warm place until double, about 2 hours. (Dough is ready if indentation remains when touched.)

Line 2 cookie sheets with aluminum foil; grease. Punch down dough. Turn onto lightly floured surface; knead until smooth. Shape into roll, 10 inches long; cut into 10 slices. Shape each slice into smooth ball. Place on foil-covered cookie sheets; flatten into circles, 3½ to 4 inches in diameter. Cover; let rise until double, about 30 minutes.

Heat oven to 375°. Brush rolls with egg. Spread Brown Sugar Glaze on centers of rolls. Make diagonal or crisscross cuts in tops of rolls with tip of sharp knife. Bake until rolls are brown and sound hollow when tapped, 20 to 25 minutes. Immediately remove rolls; cool on wire racks.

10 rolls

PER SERVING: Calories 410; Protein 9 g; Carbohydrate 75 g; Fat 8 g; Cholesterol 20 mg; Sodium 440 mg

Brown Sugar Glaze

½ **cup packed dark brown sugar**
2 **to 3 teaspoons water**

Mix brown sugar and water until of spreading consistency.

3

Poultry and Seafood

Arroz con Pollo

A real Mexican classic—chicken with rice.

2½- to 3-pound broiler-fryer chicken,
   cut up
¾ teaspoon salt
¼ to ½ teaspoon paprika
¼ teaspoon pepper
2½ cups chicken broth
1 cup uncooked regular rice
1 medium onion, chopped (about ½ cup)
1 teaspoon garlic salt
½ teaspoon dried oregano leaves
⅛ teaspoon ground turmeric
1 bay leaf, crumbled
1 package (10 ounces) frozen green
   peas, thawed and drained
Pimiento strips
Pitted ripe olives

Heat oven to 350°. Place chicken, skin sides up,
in ungreased rectangular baking dish, 13 × 9 ×
2 inches. Sprinkle with salt, paprika and pepper.
Bake uncovered 30 minutes.

Heat broth to boiling. Remove chicken and drain
fat from dish. Mix broth, rice, onion, garlic salt,
oregano, turmeric, bay leaf and peas in baking
dish. Top with chicken; cover with aluminum foil.
Cook in oven until rice and thickest pieces of
chicken are done and liquid is absorbed, about
30 minutes. Garnish with pimiento strips and
olives. **6 servings**

PER SERVING: Calories 345; Protein 29 g; Carbohydrate 32 g; Fat 11 g; Cholesterol 70 mg; Sodium 950 mg

Mexican Foods

The Mexican climate, along with the different influences in its long history, makes the
cuisine of Mexico one of the most bountiful
and varied in the world. Nearly every fruit
and vegetable can be grown there, and its
unusually long coastline yields many kinds
of fish and shellfish. Even the turkey is native to Mexico. In northern Mexico, chicken
and tortillas made of wheat are popular. As
you travel south, pork, beef, corn and fruits
become more prominent; but everywhere,
beans are a mainstay of the national diet.

Mexican Chicken

3 tablespoons vegetable oil
3- to 3½-pound broiler-fryer chicken,
** cut up**
½ cup all-purpose flour
2½ cups chicken broth
1½ to 2 teaspoons chile powder
½ teaspoon salt
⅛ teaspoon pepper
Dash of ground red pepper (cayenne)
1 medium onion, chopped (about ½ cup)
1 clove garlic, finely chopped
1 can (28 ounces) whole tomatoes,
** undrained**
1 cup uncooked regular long-grain rice
1 cup frozen corn or 1 can (8 ounces)
** whole kernel corn, undrained**
1 can (8 ounces) kidney beans,
** undrained**

Heat oil in Dutch oven. Coat chicken with flour. Cook in oil over medium heat 15 to 20 minutes or until brown; drain.

Heat oven to 350°. Mix remaining ingredients except rice, corn and beans. Pour over chicken. Cover and bake 30 minutes. Stir in rice, corn and beans. Cover and bake 30 to 40 minutes or until juices of chicken run clear and rice is tender. Serve with tortilla chips if desired.

6 servings

PER SERVING: Calories 435; Protein 33 g; Carbohydrate 27 g; Fat 22 g; Cholesterol 90 mg; Sodium 915 mg

MICROWAVE DIRECTIONS: Omit oil and flour. Decrease water to 1 cup. Place chicken with thickest parts to outside edge in 3-quart microwavable casserole. Cover tightly and microwave on high 15 minutes, rotating casserole ½ turn after 5 minutes; drain. Mix remaining ingredients except corn and beans; break up tomatoes. Stir into chicken. Cover tightly and microwave on high 25 to 30 minutes, stirring every 8 minutes, until juices of chicken run clear and rice is tender. Drain corn and beans. Stir into chicken mixture. Cover tightly and microwave on high 4 to 6 minutes or until corn and beans are hot. Serve with tortilla chips if desired.

Chicken Almendrado

This one-skillet version of "almond chicken" could hardly be easier. Almonds thicken a cinnamon-chile sauce nicely.

1 medium onion, chopped (about ½ cup)
2 tablespoons margarine or butter
1 tablespoon vegetable oil
1 cup chicken broth
¼ cup slivered almonds
1 tablespoon ground red chiles
1 teaspoon vinegar
½ teaspoon sugar
½ teaspoon ground cinnamon
4 boneless chicken breast halves
Slivered almonds

Cook and stir onion in margarine and oil in 10-inch skillet until tender. Stir in broth, ¼ cup almonds, the ground red chiles, vinegar, sugar and cinnamon. Heat to boiling; reduce heat. Simmer uncovered 10 minutes.

Spoon mixture into blender container; cover and blend on low speed until smooth, about 1 minute. Return sauce to skillet.

Dip chicken breasts into sauce to coat both sides. Place skin sides up in single layer in skillet. Heat to boiling; reduce heat. Cover and simmer until done, about 45 minutes. Serve sauce over chicken; sprinkle with almonds.

4 servings

PER SERVING: Calories 340; Protein 31 g; Carbohydrate 7 g; Fat 21 g; Cholesterol 65 mg; Sodium 320 mg

Chicken Almendrado

Mexican Fried Chicken

Many Mexican recipes are based on fresh lime marinades. Here, chicken steeps in a piquant mixture of garlic and lime juice, then is coated with chile-flecked flour and fried until golden brown and crisp.

1 clove garlic
½ teaspoon salt
2½- to 3-pound broiler-fryer chicken, cut up
¼ cup lime juice
1 small onion, finely chopped (about ¼ cup)
Vegetable oil
½ cup all-purpose flour
1 teaspoon salt
1 teaspoon chile powder

Mash garlic and ½ teaspoon salt to a paste. Rub chicken with garlic mixture. Arrange chicken in shallow glass or plastic dish. Sprinkle with lime juice and onion. Cover and refrigerate, turning occasionally, at least 3 hours. Remove chicken from marinade; pat dry.

Heat oil (¼ inch) in skillet until hot. Decrease heat to medium. Mix flour, 1 teaspoon salt and the chile powder. Coat chicken with flour mixture. Place chicken in skillet, skin sides down. Cover and cook 5 minutes. Uncover and cook 15 minutes. Turn chicken. Cover and cook 5 minutes longer. Uncover and cook until thickest pieces are done, 10 to 15 minutes; drain.

6 servings

PER SERVING: Calories 305; Protein 24 g; Carbohydrate 10 g; Fat 19 g; Cholesterol 70 mg; Sodium 600 mg

Chicken Cilantro

Cilantro is also known as Mexican parsley or coriander.

1 small onion, chopped (about ¼ cup)
1 clove garlic, finely chopped
2 tablespoons margarine or butter
2 tablespoons vegetable oil
4 chicken breasts, boned, skinned and cut into 1-inch pieces
1 teaspoon salt
¼ teaspoon pepper
2 tablespoons snipped cilantro

Cook and stir onion and garlic in margarine and oil in 10-inch skillet until onion is tender. Add chicken, salt and pepper. Cook and stir over medium-high heat until done, about 5 minutes; stir in cilantro. Pour pan juices over chicken to serve. Garnish with lemon wedges if desired.

4 servings

PER SERVING: Calories 250; Protein 26 g; Carbohydrate 1 g; Fat 16 g; Cholesterol 65 mg; Sodium 660 mg

Chicken Tostadas

6 tostada shells (6 inches in diameter)
1 can (16 ounces) refried beans or Refried Beans (page 20)
1½ cups cut-up cooked chicken
1 teaspoon chile powder
½ teaspoon dried oregano leaves
½ teaspoon salt
¼ teaspoon ground cumin
1 can (8 ounces) tomato sauce
1 medium avocado
Lemon juice
¾ cup shredded Cheddar or Monterey
   Jack cheese (about 3 ounces)
2 medium tomatoes, sliced
3 cups shredded lettuce
Sour cream
Hot taco sauce

Heat tostada shells as directed on package.
Heat beans over medium heat until hot. Heat
chicken, chile powder, oregano, salt, cumin and
tomato sauce until hot. Cut avocado lengthwise
into slices; sprinkle with lemon juice.

Spread about ¼ cup of the beans on each tostada shell; spread with about ¼ cup chicken mixture. Sprinkle 2 tablespoons cheese over each.
Arrange tomato and avocado slices and lettuce
on top. Serve with sour cream and taco
sauce. **6 tostadas**

PER SERVING: Calories 515; Protein 33 g; Carbohydrate 39 g; Fat 25 g; Cholesterol 80 mg; Sodium 1150 mg

NOTE: If desired, tostadas can be broiled after
sprinkling with cheese. Set oven control to broil
and/or 550°. Broil tostadas with tops 2 to 3
inches from heat just until cheese is melted, 1
to 2 minutes. Top with tomato and avocado
slices and shredded lettuce.

Chicken Tacos

2 cups cut-up cooked chicken
¾ teaspoon salt
1 can (4 ounces) chopped green chiles,
   drained
1 small onion, sliced
2 tablespoons vegetable oil
10 taco shells
1 small avocado
Lemon juice
½ teaspoon salt
1 cup shredded Monterey Jack or Cheddar cheese (about 4 ounces)
2 cups shredded lettuce
⅓ cup sliced pimiento-stuffed olives
Taco sauce
Sour cream

Heat chicken, ¾ teaspoon salt, the chiles and
onion in oil in 10-inch skillet over medium heat,
stirring occasionally, until chicken is hot. Heat
taco shells as directed on package. Cut avocado
lengthwise into slices; sprinkle with lemon juice
and ½ teaspoon salt.

Spoon about ¼ cup chicken mixture into each
shell. Top with cheese, lettuce, olives and avocado. Serve with taco sauce and sour
cream. **5 servings (2 tacos each)**

PER SERVING: Calories 620; Protein 43 g; Carbohydrate 27 g; Fat 38 g; Cholesterol 125 mg; Sodium 1560 mg

Mexican Chicken Manicotti

Mexican Chicken Manicotti

8 uncooked manicotti shells
1½ cups cut-up cooked chicken or turkey (about 8 ounces)
1 cup shredded carrot (about 2 medium)
1 cup low-fat ricotta cheese
2 tablespoons sliced green onions (with tops)
2 tablespoons snipped fresh or 2 teaspoons dried cilantro
1 clove garlic, finely chopped
1 cup salsa
¼ cup shredded Monterey Jack cheese with jalapeño peppers (1 ounce)

Heat oven to 325°. Cook manicotti shells as directed on package; drain. Mix chicken, carrot, ricotta cheese, onions, cilantro and garlic. Fill manicotti shells with chicken mixture.

Arrange in ungreased rectangular pan, 13 × 9 × 2 inches. Pour salsa over manicotti; sprinkle with Monterey Jack cheese. Cover and bake about 35 minutes or until hot in center.

4 servings

PER SERVING: Calories 350; Protein 29 g; Carbohydrate 32 g; Fat 12 g; Cholesterol 75 mg; Sodium 180 mg

Stuffed Peppers

3 large bell peppers (green, red or yellow)
½ pound ground turkey, cooked and drained
1 cup cooked rice
¼ cup chopped onion (about 1 small)
1 teaspoon ground cumin
½ teaspoon salt
¼ teaspoon pepper
2 eggs
2 cloves garlic, finely chopped
1 can (4 ounces) chopped green chiles
1 jar (2 ounces) diced pimientos, drained
½ cup shredded Monterey Jack cheese

Heat oven to 350°. Cut bell peppers lengthwise into halves. Remove seeds and membranes; rinse peppers. Cook 2 minutes in enough boiling water to cover; drain. Mix remaining ingredients except cheese; loosely stuff each pepper half. Arrange peppers in rectangular baking dish, 12 × 7½ × 2 inches, sprayed with nonstick cooking spray. Cover and bake until rice mixture is hot, about 30 minutes. Uncover; sprinkle with cheese. Bake until cheese is melted, about 5 minutes longer.

6 servings

PER SERVING: Calories 175; Protein 13 g; Carbohydrate 15 g; Fat 7 g; Cholesterol 110 mg; Sodium 410 mg

MICROWAVE DIRECTIONS: Prepare peppers as directed. Cover with plastic wrap, folding back one corner to vent, and microwave on high 6 minutes; rotate dish ½ turn. Sprinkle with cheese. Microwave uncovered until rice mixture is hot and cheese is melted, 1 to 3 minutes longer.

Chipotle Fettuccine

Chipotle Fettuccine

Three ingredients found in Mexican cooking (corn, chiles and smoked meat) are incorporated here in a contemporary dish. Adding ground or finely chopped chiles to any homemade pasta heightens both the color and flavor of the finished dish. Chipotle in adobo sauce adds a smokey note all its own.

Chipotle Fettuccine (right)
1½ cups whole kernel corn
½ cup water
1 small onion, chopped (about ¼ cup)
2 tablespoons margarine or butter
2 tablespoons all-purpose flour
½ teaspoon salt
¼ teaspoon pepper
1 cup milk
½ cup half-and-half
**2 cups cut-up smoked turkey breast
(about 12 ounces)**

Prepare Chipotle Fettuccine. Heat corn, water and onion to boiling; reduce heat. Cover and simmer 5 minutes. Pour into food processor workbowl fitted with steel blade or into blender container; cover and process until almost smooth.

Heat margarine in 2-quart saucepan over low heat until melted. Stir in flour, salt and pepper. Cook over low heat, stirring constantly, until smooth and bubbly. Remove from heat; stir in corn mixture, milk, half-and-half and turkey. Heat to boiling, stirring constantly. Boil and stir 1 minute.

Break fettuccine into desired-size pieces. Cook fettuccine in 3 quarts boiling salted water (1 tablespoon salt) until tender, 8 to 10 minutes; drain. Toss with turkey mixture.

6 servings

PER SERVING: Calories 420; Protein 27 g; Carbohydrate 46 g; Fat 14 g; Cholesterol 125 mg; Sodium 840 mg

Chipotle Fettuccine

2 cups all-purpose flour
½ teaspoon salt
1 tablespoon vegetable oil
2 eggs
1 to 2 canned chipotle chiles in adobo sauce, finely chopped

Mix flour and salt in large bowl; make well in center. Beat oil, eggs and chiles; pour into well. Stir with fork, gradually bringing flour mixture to center, until dough forms a ball. If dough is too dry, mix in up to 2 tablespoons water. Roll and cut as directed below. (Use additional flour when rolling and cutting noodles.) Place fettuccine strips on towel; let stand 30 minutes.

Hand-Rolling Method: Knead dough on lightly floured surface until smooth and elastic, about 5 minutes. Divide into 4 equal parts. Roll dough, one part at a time, into paper-thin rectangle, about 14 × 10 inches (keep remaining dough covered). Loosely fold rectangle lengthwise into thirds; cut crosswise into ¼-inch strips. Unfold, and separate strips.

Manual Pasta Machine Method: Knead dough on a lightly floured surface about 2 to 3 minutes. Divide dough into 4 equal parts. Feed dough, one part at a time, through smooth rollers set at widest setting (keep remaining dough covered). Sprinkle with flour if dough becomes sticky. Fold lengthwise into thirds. Repeat feeding dough through rollers and folding into thirds until dough is firm and smooth, 8 to 10 times. Feed dough through progressively narrower settings until dough is paper thin. (Dough will lengthen as it becomes thinner; it may be cut crosswise at any time for easier handling.) Feed through fettuccine-cutting rollers.

South American Roast Turkey

Tangy olives, spicy pork sausage and fresh, sweet peaches cook to moist perfection inside this bird. A creamy giblet gravy adds an elegant touch to this Latin American specialty.

1 medium onion, chopped (about ½ cup)
1 pound bulk sweet Italian sausage
2 eggs
4 cups soft bread crumbs
¼ cup chopped pimiento-stuffed olives
2 large peaches, peeled and coarsely chopped, or 1 package (16 ounces) frozen unsweetened peach slices, thawed and coarsely chopped
1 teaspoon dried oregano leaves
½ teaspoon salt
¼ teaspoon pepper
12-pound turkey, giblets and neck reserved
Olive oil
Gravy (right)

Cook and stir onion and sausage in 10-inch skillet over medium heat until sausage is brown; drain. Beat eggs with fork in 2½-quart bowl. Add sausage mixture, bread crumbs, olives, peaches, oregano, salt and pepper; toss.

Remove giblets and neck from turkey; prepare for Gravy. Fill wishbone area of turkey with stuffing. Fasten neck skin to back with skewer. Fold wings across back with tips touching. Fill body cavity lightly. (Do not pack—stuffing will expand during cooking.) Tuck drumsticks under band of skin at tail, or tie or skewer to tail.

Place turkey, breast side up, on rack in shallow roasting pan. Insert meat thermometer so tip is in thickest part of inside thigh muscle or thickest part of breast meat and does not touch bone. Brush with oil. Roast in 325° oven, brushing with pan juices every 45 minutes, until meat thermometer registers 185°, 3½ to 4 hours. Let turkey stand 20 minutes before carving. Prepare Gravy; serve with turkey. As soon as possible after serving, remove every bit of stuffing from the turkey. Cool stuffing and turkey promptly, refrigerate separately, and use within two days. **14 servings**

PER SERVING: Calories 798; Protein 67 g; Carbohydrate 30 g; Fat 43 g; Cholesterol 233 mg; Sodium 907 mg

Gravy

Giblets and neck of turkey
2 cups water
½ teaspoon salt
⅔ cup turkey drippings (fat and juices)
⅔ cup all-purpose flour
½ cup half-and-half
Salt and pepper to taste

Heat giblets, neck, water and ½ teaspoon salt to boiling; reduce heat. Cover and simmer 30 minutes. Remove giblets and neck; chop giblets and discard neck. Reserve broth for gravy. (Cover and refrigerate giblets and broth if not using immediately.)

Pour and scrape all drippings from roasting pan. Pour ⅔ cup drippings into 3-quart saucepan; stir in flour. Cook over low heat, stirring constantly, until mixture is thick and bubbly; remove from heat. Stir in reserved broth, the half-and-half and chopped giblets. Heat to boiling, stirring constantly; boil and stir 1 minute. Stir in salt and pepper.

Spicy Turkey–Tortilla Casserole

Oregano, cumin, and red pepper perk up ground turkey in this layered casserole. For timid taste buds, you can omit the red pepper, since the Green Sauce adds a little kick of its own.

1 pound ground turkey
½ cup chopped onion (about 1 medium)
¼ cup white wine vinegar
1 tablespoon snipped fresh or 1 teaspoon dried oregano leaves
1 teaspoon paprika
½ teaspoon salt
½ teaspoon ground cumin
¼ teaspoon crushed red pepper
1 clove garlic, finely chopped
1 cup Green Sauce (page 11)
½ cup low-fat sour cream
½ cup chicken broth
8 corn tortillas (6 inches in diameter), cut into ½-inch strips
½ cup shredded low-fat Cheddar cheese (2 ounces)

Heat oven to 350°. Spray 10-inch nonstick skillet with nonstick cooking spray. Cook turkey, onion, vinegar, oregano, paprika, salt, cumin, red pepper and garlic in skillet over medium heat, stirring constantly, until turkey is brown.

Prepare Green Sauce and spread ½ cup in bottom of ungreased square baking dish, 8 × 8 × 2 inches. Mix remaining Green Sauce, the sour cream and broth. Layer half each of the tortilla strips, turkey mixture and sour cream mixture on Green Sauce in dish; repeat. Sprinkle with cheese. Bake uncovered about 25 minutes or until hot and bubbly.   **4 servings**

PER SERVING: Calories 435; Protein 33 g; Carbohydrate 29 g; Fat 20 g; Cholesterol 85 mg; Sodium 920 mg

MICROWAVE DIRECTIONS: Decrease chicken broth to ¼ cup. Crumble turkey into 2-quart microwavable casserole. Stir in onion, vinegar, oregano, paprika, salt, cumin, red pepper and garlic. Cover loosely and microwave on high 3 to 5 minutes, stirring every 2 minutes, until turkey is no longer pink. Spread ½ cup of the Green Sauce in bottom of square microwavable dish, 8 × 8 × 2 inches. Mix remaining Green Sauce, the sour cream and broth. Layer half each of the tortilla strips, turkey mixture and sour cream mixture on Green Sauce in dish; repeat. Sprinkle with cheese. Cover loosely and microwave on high 6 to 8 minutes, rotating dish ¼ turn every 2 minutes, until center is hot. Let stand covered 5 minutes.

Turkey with Southwest Stuffing

This rich corn bread stuffing boasts an untraditional, delicious combination of sage, cilantro, and pecans. Chayote squash guarantees that it will be moist.

Southwest Stuffing (right)
10- to 12-pound turkey
Margarine or butter, melted

Prepare Southwest Stuffing. Fill wishbone area of turkey with stuffing. Fasten neck skin to back with skewer. Fold wings across back with tips touching. Fill body cavity lightly. (Do not pack—stuffing will expand.) Tuck drumsticks under band of skin at tail, or skewer to tail.

Spoon any remaining stuffing into ungreased 1-quart casserole; cover. (Refrigerate until about 30 minutes before turkey is done. Bake covered until hot, about 45 minutes.)

Heat oven to 325°. Place turkey, breast side up, on rack in shallow roasting pan. Brush with margarine. Insert meat thermometer so tip is in thickest part of inside thigh muscle or thickest part of breast meat and does not touch bone. (Tip of thermometer can be inserted in center of stuffing.) Do not add water. Do not cover. Roast until done, 3½ to 4 hours.

Place a tent of aluminum foil loosely over turkey when it begins to turn golden. After 2½ hours, cut band or remove skewer holding legs. Turkey is done when thermometer placed in thigh muscle registers 185° or drumstick meat feels very soft when pressed between fingers. (Thermometer inserted in stuffing will register 165°.)

Let stand about 20 minutes before carving. As soon as possible after serving, remove every bit of stuffing from turkey. Cool stuffing and turkey promptly; refrigerate separately, and use within 2 days.   **12 servings**

PER SERVING: Calories 926; Protein 60 g; Carbohydrate 40 g; Fat 57 g; Cholesterol 199 mg; Sodium 938 mg

Southwest Stuffing

1 cup chopped chayote (about 1 small)
4 jalapeño chiles, seeded and finely chopped
2 cloves garlic, finely chopped
1 large onion, finely chopped (about 1 cup)
1 cup margarine or butter
1 tablespoon snipped fresh cilantro
1 teaspoon salt
½ teaspoon dried thyme leaves
½ teaspoon dried sage leaves
9 cups ½-inch cubes corn bread
1 cup chopped pecans

Cook and stir chayote, chiles, garlic and onion in margarine in 10-inch skillet until chayote is tender. Stir in cilantro, salt, thyme and sage until well blended. Stir in about ⅓ of the corn bread cubes. Turn mixture into deep bowl. Add remaining corn bread cubes and the pecans; toss.

Turkey with Southwest Stuffing

Turkey Fajitas

1 tablespoon lime juice
¼ teaspoon crushed red pepper
1 clove garlic, crushed
12 ounces cooked turkey, cut into about
    2-inch strips (about 2 cups)
8 flour tortillas (7 inches in diameter)
1 tablespoon vegetable oil
1 container (6 ounces) frozen guacamole,
    thawed or Guacamole (page 1)
1 jar (10 to 12 ounces) chunky red salsa

Heat oven to 325°. Mix lime juice, red pepper
and garlic in glass or plastic bowl. Stir in turkey
until well coated. Cover and refrigerate.

Wrap tortillas in aluminum foil; heat in oven
about 15 minutes or until warm.

Heat oil in wok or 10-inch skillet over medium-
high heat. Sauté turkey in oil about 2 minutes,
stirring frequently, until turkey is hot.

Divide the turkey and guacamole among the tortillas. Top each with 2 tablespoons salsa. Fold
1 end of tortillas up about 1 inch over turkey
mixture; fold right and left sides over folded
ends, overlapping. Fold down remaining ends.
Serve with remaining salsa.   **4 servings**

PER SERVING: Calories 525; Protein 33 g; Carbohydrate 56 g; Fat 19 g; Cholesterol 75 mg; Sodium 1320 mg

Turkey–Vegetable Chile

½ cup chopped green bell pepper
¼ cup chopped onion (about 1 small)
2 cloves garlic, finely chopped
2 teaspoons olive or vegetable oil
3 cups cut-up cooked turkey or chicken
½ cup water
1 tablespoon snipped fresh or 1 tea-
    spoon dried oregano leaves
1 tablespoon chile powder
1 teaspoon ground cumin
½ teaspoon salt
1 can (16 ounces) whole tomatoes,
    undrained
1 package (10 ounces) frozen mixed
    vegetables
2 cups ½-inch zucchini slices (about 2
    medium)

Cook and stir bell pepper, onion and garlic in oil
in 3-quart saucepan over medium heat until
onion is tender, about 3 minutes. Stir in remaining ingredients except frozen vegetables
and zucchini; break up tomatoes. Heat to boiling;
reduce heat. Cover and simmer 1 hour, stirring
occasionally.

Stir in frozen vegetables and zucchini. Heat to
boiling; reduce heat. Simmer uncovered, stirring
occasionally, until zucchini is crisp-tender, about
5 minutes.   **6 servings, about 1 cup each**

PER SERVING: Calories 200; Protein 24 g; Carbohydrate 13 g; Fat 6 g; Cholesterol 55 mg; Sodium 510 mg

MICROWAVE DIRECTIONS: Mix bell pepper, onion,
garlic and oil in 3-quart microwavable casserole.
Cover tightly and microwave on high 3 minutes.
Stir in remaining ingredients except frozen vegetables and zucchini; break up tomatoes. Cover
and microwave 15 minutes. Stir in frozen vegetables; cover and microwave 10 minutes. Stir in
zucchini; cover and microwave until zucchini is
crisp-tender, 3 to 6 minutes longer.

Fish with Green Chiles

1 pound lean fish fillets
1 medium onion, thinly sliced
1 tablespoon olive or vegetable oil
¼ teaspoon salt
¼ teaspoon coarsely ground pepper
1 can (4 ounces) chopped green chiles,
  drained
12 pimiento-stuffed olives
¼ cup dry white wine
1 tablespoon lemon juice
Lemon wedges

If fish fillets are large, cut into 4 serving pieces. Place onion in oil in 10-inch nonstick skillet. Place fish on onion; sprinkle with salt and pepper. Spoon chiles over fish; top with olives. Mix wine and lemon juice; pour over fish. Heat to boiling; reduce heat. Cover and simmer until fish flakes easily with fork, about 10 minutes. Serve with lemon wedges.   **4 servings**

PER SERVING: Calories 170; Protein 19 g; Carbohydrate 5 g; Fat 8 g; Cholesterol 35 mg; Sodium 430 mg

---

MICROWAVE DIRECTIONS: Omit oil. Arrange onion in square microwavable dish, 8 × 8 × 2 inches; place fish on onion, thickest parts to outside edges. Sprinkle with salt and pepper. Spoon chiles over fish; top with olives. Mix 3 tablespoons wine and lemon juice; pour over fish. Cover with plastic wrap, folding back one corner to vent, and microwave on high 4 minutes; rotate dish ½ turn. Microwave until fish flakes easily with fork, 3 to 5 minutes longer. Let stand covered 3 minutes. Serve with lemon wedges.

Baked Fish, Spanish Style

A colorful array of bright vegetables and lemon slices make this simple dish distinctly Spanish and shows a part of the heritage of Mexico.

1½ pounds fish steaks or fillets
1½ teaspoons salt
¼ teaspoon paprika
¼ teaspoon pepper
1 medium green bell pepper, cut into
  rings
1 medium tomato, sliced
1 small onion, sliced
2 tablespoons lemon juice
2 tablespoons olive or vegetable oil
1 clove garlic, finely chopped
Lemon wedges

Heat oven to 375°. If fish pieces are large, cut into serving pieces. Arrange fish in ungreased square baking dish, 8 × 8 × 2 inches; sprinkle with salt, paprika and pepper. Top with bell pepper rings and tomato and onion slices. Mix lemon juice, oil and garlic; pour over fish. Cover and bake 15 minutes. Uncover and bake until fish flakes easily with fork, 10 to 15 minutes longer. Garnish with lemon wedges.

6 servings

PER SERVING: Calories 160; Protein 22 g; Carbohydrate 4 g; Fat 6 g; Cholesterol 60 mg; Sodium 630 mg

Red Snapper, Vera Cruz Style

Lemon, tomatoes and pimiento-stuffed-olives accent this entrée from Mexico's principal seaport.

- 2 pounds red snapper fillets
- 2 tablespoons capers
- 1 tablespoon lemon juice
- 1 jar (2 ounces) pimiento-stuffed green olives, drained
- 1 large onion, chopped
- 1 clove garlic, finely chopped
- 2 tablespoons vegetable oil
- 1 can (28 ounces) whole tomatoes, drained and chopped
- 1/2 teaspoon salt
- 1/8 teaspoon pepper

If fish fillets are large, cut into serving pieces. Arrange fish in lightly oiled oblong baking dish, 13 × 9 × 2 inches. Sprinkle with capers, lemon juice and olives.

Heat oven to 350°. Cook and stir onion and garlic in oil in 10-inch skillet over medium heat until onion is tender; add tomatoes, salt and pepper. Heat to boiling; reduce heat. Simmer uncovered, stirring occasionally, 5 minutes. Spoon tomato mixture evenly over fish. Bake uncovered until fish flakes easily with fork, 25 to 30 minutes. Serve with lemon wedges if desired.

6 servings

PER SERVING: Calories 225; Protein 30 g; Carbohydrate 8 g; Fat 8 g; Cholesterol 80 mg; Sodium 750 mg

Shrimp Fajitas

- 8 flour tortillas (7 or 8 inches in diameter)
- 1 tablespoon vegetable oil
- 1 pound raw medium peeled and deveined shrimp
- 1 tablespoon lime juice
- 1 1/2 teaspoons chopped fresh or 1/2 teaspoon dried oregano leaves
- 1/4 teaspoon ground cumin
- 1 clove garlic, finely chopped
- 1 cup salsa or Fresh Tomato Salsa (page 11)
- 1 cup guacamole or Guacamole (page 1)

Heat oven to 250°. Wrap tortillas in aluminum foil or place on heatproof serving plate and cover with aluminum foil. Heat in oven for about 15 minutes or until warm.

Heat oil in 10-inch skillet over medium heat. Add shrimp, lime juice, oregano, cumin and garlic. Cook about 5 minutes, stirring constantly, until shrimp are pink.

Divide shrimp evenly among tortillas. Top with salsa and guacamole. Fold one end of tortilla up about 1 inch over shrimp mixture. Fold right and left sides over folded end, overlapping. Fold down remaining end. Serve with extra salsa and guacamole if desired.

4 servings

PER SERVING: Calories 470; Protein 25 g; Carbohydrate 57 g; Fat 16 g; Cholesterol 170 mg; Sodium 1390 mg

---

Working with Chiles and Peppers

The flesh, ribs and seeds of chiles are rich in irritating, burning oils. When preparing chiles, always wash hands and utensils in soapy water. Be careful not to rub your face—eyes especially—until the oils have been thoroughly washed away. Some cooks who work with chiles for any extended length of time wear plastic gloves.

Hot Salsa Cod

Prepare the spicy salsa ahead of time and serve it cold, if you like.

Hot Salsa (right)
1 pound cod or lean fish fillets
1 tablespoon reduced-calorie margarine, melted
1 tablespoon finely snipped fresh or 1 teaspoon dried cilantro leaves, if desired
1/4 teaspoon salt
1 clove garlic, crushed

Prepare Hot Salsa. Set oven control to broil. If fish fillets are large, cut into 4 serving pieces. Place on rack sprayed with nonstick cooking spray in broiler pan. Mix margarine, cilantro, salt and garlic; brush half of the mixture over fish. Broil with tops about 4 inches from heat until light brown, about 6 minutes.

Turn fish carefully; brush with remaining margarine mixture. Broil until fish flakes easily with fork, 4 to 6 minutes longer. Serve with Hot Salsa; garnish with lime wedges if desired.

4 servings

PER SERVING: Calories 165; Protein 20 g; Carbohydrate 6 g; Fat 7 g; Cholesterol 35 mg; Sodium 270 mg

Hot Salsa

1 1/2 cups finely chopped tomatoes (about 2 medium)
1/2 cup chopped onion (about 1 medium)
1 tablespoon finely snipped fresh or 1 teaspoon dried cilantro leaves, if desired
1 tablespoon lemon juice
1 teaspoon vegetable oil
1/2 teaspoon dried oregano leaves
3 cloves garlic, crushed
1 canned jalapeño chile, seeded and finely chopped

Heat all ingredients over medium heat, stirring occasionally, until hot and bubbly, about 5 minutes.

MICROWAVE DIRECTIONS: Arrange fish, thickest parts to outside edges, in square microwavable dish, 8 × 8 × 2 inches. Mix margarine, cilantro, salt and garlic; brush over fish. Cover with plastic wrap, folding back one corner to vent, and microwave on high 3 minutes; rotate dish 1/2 turn. Microwave until fish flakes easily with fork, 3 to 5 minutes longer. Let stand covered 3 minutes.

Mix all ingredients for Hot Salsa in 4-cup microwavable measure. Cover with plastic wrap, folding back one corner to vent, and microwave on high 2 minutes; stir. Microwave until hot and bubbly, 2 to 3 minutes longer. Drain if desired. Serve with fish; garnish with lime wedges if desired.

Grilled Shrimp

Grilled Shrimp

If you like, serve this tangy shrimp with hot rice.

1/4 cup vegetable oil
1/4 cup tequila or lime juice
1/4 cup red wine vinegar
2 tablespoons lime juice
1 tablespoon ground red chiles
1/2 teaspoon salt
2 cloves garlic, finely chopped
1 red bell pepper, finely chopped
24 large raw shrimp, peeled and deveined (leave tails intact)

Mix all ingredients except shrimp in shallow glass or plastic dish; stir in shrimp. Cover and refrigerate 1 hour.

Remove shrimp from marinade; reserve marinade. Thread 4 shrimp on each of six 8-inch metal skewers. Grill over medium coals, turning once, until pink, 2 to 3 minutes on each side.

Heat marinade to boiling in nonaluminum saucepan; reduce heat to low. Simmer uncovered until bell pepper is tender, about 5 minutes. Serve with shrimp.   **6 servings**

PER SERVING: Calories 115; Protein 6 g; Carbohydrate 3 g; Fat 9 g; Cholesterol 55 mg; Sodium 240 mg

BROILED SHRIMP: Set oven control to broil. Place skewered shrimp on rack in broiler pan. Broil with tops about 4 inches from heat, turning once, until pink, 2 to 3 minutes on each side.

Skillet Paella

1 package (12 ounces) frozen peeled shrimp
1 package (10 ounces) frozen green peas
1 can (16 ounces) whole tomatoes, undrained
1 can (6 1/2 ounces) minced clams, drained
2 cups uncooked instant rice
1/2 cup cut-up cooked chicken or 1 can (5 ounces) chunk chicken, drained
2 tablespoons instant minced onion
1 teaspoon instant chicken bouillon
1 teaspoon paprika
1/4 teaspoon ground red pepper (cayenne)
1/8 teaspoon saffron

Rinse frozen shrimp and peas with cold water to separate; drain. Mix all ingredients in 12-inch skillet; break up tomatoes. Heat to boiling, stirring occasionally; reduce heat. Simmer uncovered 5 minutes; remove from heat. Cover tightly and let stand about 10 minutes.

4 servings

PER SERVING: Calories 350; Protein 26 g; Carbohydrate 54 g; Fat 4 g; Cholesterol 155 mg; Sodium 640 mg

Scallops with Red Pepper Sauce

Scallops with Red Pepper Sauce

1 large red bell pepper, cut into fourths
⅛ teaspoon salt
10 drops red pepper sauce
1 clove garlic, finely chopped
¼ cup plain nonfat yogurt
1 pound bay scallops
¼ cup sliced green onions (with tops)
Freshly snipped cilantro leaves

Place steamer basket in ½ inch water in saucepan or skillet (water should not touch bottom of basket). Place bell pepper in basket. Cover tightly and heat to boiling; reduce heat. Steam 8 to 10 minutes or until tender.

Place bell pepper, salt, pepper sauce and garlic in blender or food processor. Cover and blend on medium speed until almost smooth. Heat in 1-quart saucepan over medium heat, stirring occasionally, until hot; remove from heat. Gradually stir in yogurt; keep warm.

Spray 10-inch nonstick skillet with nonstick cooking spray. Heat over medium-high heat. Add scallops and onions; stir-fry 4 to 5 minutes or until scallops are white in center. Serve sauce with scallops. Garnish with cilantro.

4 servings

PER SERVING: Calories 115; Protein 20 g; Carbohydrate 6 g; Fat 1 g; Cholesterol 35 mg; Sodium 270 mg

MICROWAVE DIRECTIONS: Prepare bell pepper and place in 1-quart microwavable casserole. Add ¼ cup water. Cover tightly and microwave on high 4 to 5 minutes, stirring after 2 minutes, until tender; drain. Blend as directed. Pour into 1-quart microwavable casserole. Cover tightly and microwave on high 30 to 60 seconds or until hot. Stir in yogurt. Mix scallops and onions in 1½-quart microwavable casserole. Cover tightly and microwave on high 4 to 6 minutes, stirring every 2 minutes, until scallops are white in center; drain.

Southwest Scallops

Can't find Anaheim chiles? Use a small red bell pepper. It will also give the sauce a milder and sweeter flavor.

1 red Anaheim chile, chopped
¼ cup sliced green onions (with tops)
2 tablespoons reduced-calorie margarine
2 tablespoons lime juice
2 pounds sea scallops
2 cups cubed fresh pineapple
1 cup Chinese pea pod halves (about 3 ounces)
3 cups hot cooked fettuccine

Cook chile, onions, margarine and lime juice in 10-inch skillet, stirring occasionally, until margarine is melted. Carefully stir in scallops. Cook over medium heat about 12 minutes, stirring frequently, until scallops are white. Stir in pineapple and pea pods. Heat until hot. Remove scallop mixture with slotted spoon; keep warm.

Heat liquid in skillet to boiling. Boil until slightly thickened and reduced to about half. Spoon scallop mixture onto fettuccine; pour liquid over scallop mixture.

6 servings

PER SERVING: Calories 335; Protein 39 g; Carbohydrate 34 g; Fat 6 g; Cholesterol 80 mg; Sodium 430 mg

Santa Fe Flank Steak

4

Meaty and Meatless Entrées

Sante Fe Flank Steak

3 guajillo chiles
2 cloves garlic, finely chopped
1 tablespoon packed brown sugar
1 teaspoon dried thyme leaves
¼ teaspoon salt
¼ teaspoon freshly ground pepper
2 pounds beef flank steak

Place chilies and enough water to cover chiles in 2-quart saucepan. Heat to boiling. Boil uncovered 5 minutes; drain. Remove stems; finely chop chiles. Mix chiles and remaining ingredients except beef steak. Rub mixture on both sides of beef. Cover and refrigerate 1 hour.

Set oven control to broil. Place beef on rack in broiler pan. Broil with top about 3 inches from heat until brown, about 5 minutes. Turn beef; broil until of medium-rare doneness, 4 to 6 minutes longer. Cut beef diagonally across grain into very thin slices.   **8 servings**

PER SERVING: Calories 190; Protein 25 g; Carbohydrate 4 g; Fat 8 g; Cholesterol 65 mg; Sodium 130 mg

Fajitas

Fajitas are fun to make—and eat!

1½ pounds beef boneless sirloin steak,
  about 1½ inches thick
¼ cup vegetable oil
¼ cup red wine vinegar
1 teaspoon sugar
1 teaspoon dried oregano leaves
1 teaspoon chile powder
½ teaspoon garlic powder
½ teaspoon salt
¼ teaspoon pepper
10 large flour tortillas
2 large onions, sliced
2 medium green or red bell peppers, cut
  into ¼-inch strips
2 tablespoons vegetable oil
1 cup shredded Cheddar or Monterey
  Jack cheese (4 ounces)
1 jar (8 ounces) salsa or Fresh Tomato
  Salsa (page 11)
2 containers (6 ounces each) frozen guacamole, thawed
¾ cup sour cream

Trim excess fat from beef steak. Prick beef with fork in several places. Mix ¼ cup oil, the vinegar, sugar, oregano, chile powder, garlic powder, salt and pepper in ungreased square baking dish 8 × 8 × 2 inches. Place beef in dish, turning once to coat both sides. Cover and refrigerate, turning beef occasionally, at least 8 hours but no longer than 24 hours.

Heat oven to 325°. Wrap tortillas in aluminum foil and heat in oven until warm, about 15 minutes. Remove from oven; keep tortillas wrapped. Remove beef from marinade; reserve marinade. Set oven control to broil. Broil beef with top about 3 inches from heat until brown, about 8 minutes. Turn beef; brush with marinade and broil until medium doneness, 7 to 8 minutes longer. While beef broils, cook and stir onions and bell peppers in 2 tablespoons oil until crisp-tender, about 10 minutes. Slice beef diagonally into very thin slices.

For each serving, place some beef, onion mixture, cheese and salsa in center of tortilla. Fold 1 end up about 1 inch over beef mixture; fold right and left sides over folded end. Serve with guacamole and sour cream if desired.

5 servings

PER SERVING: Calories 755; Protein 48 g; Carbohydrate 60 g; Fat 36 g; Cholesterol 120 mg; Sodium 1230 mg

Tostadas

A tostada is a tortilla topped with a variety of foods. Our Tostadas include Refried Beans, ground beef, cheese, lettuce, tomatoes and avocados.

Refried Beans (right)
Vegetable oil
8 corn tortillas (6 inches in diameter)
1 pound ground beef
1 medium onion, chopped (about ½ cup)
1 clove garlic, chopped
1 can (15 ounces) tomato sauce
2 teaspoons chile powder
1 teaspoon dried oregano leaves
¼ teaspoon salt
¼ teaspoon ground cumin
¼ teaspoon crushed red pepper
1 package (8 ounces) shredded Monterey
  Jack or Cheddar cheese (2 cups)
4 cups shredded lettuce
3 medium tomatoes, sliced
1 avocado, sliced
Sour cream
1 jar (8 ounces) salsa

Prepare Refried Beans. Heat oil (¼ inch) to 360°. Fry 1 tortilla at a time until slightly brown and crisp, about 30 seconds on each side; drain. Keep warm in 200° oven no longer than 20 minutes.

Cook and stir ground beef, onion and garlic until beef is light brown; drain. Stir in tomato sauce, chile powder, oregano, salt, cumin and red pepper. Heat to boiling; reduce heat. Simmer uncovered 15 minutes.

Place ¼ to ⅓ cup beans on each tortilla; spread with about ⅓ cup meat mixture. Sprinkle each tostada with cheese and lettuce. Arrange tomato and avocado slices on top. Top with sour cream; serve with salsa.   **8 servings**

PER SERVING: Calories 585; Protein 28 g; Carbohydrate 42 g; Fat 34 g; Cholesterol 70 mg; Sodium 1140 mg

Refried Beans

 2 cups water
 8 ounces dried pinto beans (about 1¼ cups)
 1 medium onion, chopped (about ½ cup)
 1 clove garlic, chopped
 ½ teaspoon salt
 3 tablespoons melted bacon fat, melted shortening or vegetable oil

Heat water, beans, onion and garlic to boiling in 2-quart saucepan; boil 2 minutes. Remove from heat; cover and let stand 1 hour.

Add just enough water to cover beans; add salt. Heat to boiling; reduce heat. Cover and simmer, stirring occasionally, until tender, about 1½ hours. (Add water during cooking if necessary.) Mash beans; stir in bacon fat until completely absorbed.

NOTE: 1 can (about 16 ounces) refried beans can be substituted for the Refried Beans.

Layered Tostada Bake

 1 pound ground beef
 1 medium onion, chopped (about ½ cup)
 1 envelope (1¼ ounces) taco seasoning mix
 1 can (8 ounces) tomato sauce
 1 can (16 ounces) refried beans or Refried Beans (page 20)
 1 can (4 ounces) whole green chiles, drained, seeded and chopped
 ½ cup sliced pitted ripe olives
 1 cup Bisquick® original baking mix
 ½ cup cornmeal
 ¼ cup milk
 1 egg, beaten
 2 tablespoons vegetable oil
 1 cup sour cream
 1 egg
 2 cups shredded Cheddar cheese (8 ounces)

Heat oven to 375°. Grease rectangular baking dish, 12 × 7½ × 2 inches. Cook and stir ground beef and onion in 10-inch skillet until beef is brown; drain. Stir in seasoning mix, tomato sauce, beans, chiles and olives. Mix Bisquick, cornmeal, milk, beaten egg and oil until moistened; beat vigorously 30 seconds. Spread in dish. Spoon beef mixture over dough. Mix remaining ingredients; spoon over beef mixture. Bake uncovered 30 minutes. Let stand 10 minutes before cutting.   **6 servings**

PER SERVING: Calories 705; Protein 35 g; Carbohydrate 47 g; Fat 42 g; Cholesterol 180 mg; Sodium 1700 mg

Chile-stuffed Peppers

Chile-stuffed Peppers

Half of the meat in these stuffed peppers has been replaced by beans. Try substituting beans for part of the meat in your favorite casserole—it's better for you and more economical, too.

4 large red, yellow or green bell peppers
½ pound extra-lean ground beef
½ cup finely chopped onion (about
    1 medium)
2 teaspoons chile powder
½ teaspoon ground cumin
1 can (16 ounces) kidney beans, drained
1 can (15 ounces) tomato puree
1 can (4 ounces) chopped green chiles,
    undrained

Heat oven to 350°. Cut bell peppers lengthwise into halves. Remove seeds and membranes. Place peppers, cut sides up, in rectangular baking dish, 13 × 9 × 2 inches.

Cook ground beef and onion in 10-inch nonstick skillet over medium heat, stirring occasionally, until beef is brown; drain. Stir in remaining ingredients. Heat to boiling; reduce heat. Cover and simmer 10 minutes, stirring frequently.

Divide beef mixture evenly among peppers. Cover and bake 40 to 45 minutes or until peppers are tender.   **4 servings**

PER SERVING: Calories 230; Protein 21 g; Carbohydrate 31 g; Fat 4 g; Cholesterol 40 mg; Sodium 740 mg

MICROWAVE DIRECTIONS: Prepare peppers as directed—except place in rectangular microwavable dish, 13 × 9 × 2 inches. Crumble ground beef into 3-quart microwavable casserole. Add onion. Cover loosely and microwave on high 2 to 4 minutes, stirring after 2 minutes, until beef is no longer pink; drain. Stir in remaining ingredients. Cover tightly and microwave 5 to 7 minutes, stirring after 3 minutes, until boiling. Divide beef mixture evenly among peppers. Cover tightly and microwave 10 to 12 minutes, rearranging peppers after 5 minutes, until peppers are tender. Let stand covered 5 minutes.

Chile con Carne

This chile is nice topped with sour cream, salsa and grated cheese, in your favorite combination.

1 pound ground beef
1 large onion, chopped (about 1 cup)
2 cloves garlic, crushed
1 tablespoon chile powder
½ teaspoon salt
1 teaspoon ground cumin
1 teaspoon dried oregano leaves
1 teaspoon cocoa
½ teaspoon red pepper sauce
1 can (16 ounces) whole tomatoes,
    undrained
1 can (15½ ounces) red kidney beans,
    undrained

Cook ground beef, onion and garlic in 3-quart saucepan, stirring occasionally, until beef is brown; drain. Stir in remaining ingredients except beans; break up tomatoes. Heat to boiling; reduce heat. Cover and simmer 1 hour, stirring occasionally.

Stir in beans. Heat to boiling; reduce heat. Simmer uncovered about 20 minutes, stirring occasionally, until of desired thickness.

4 servings

PER SERVING: Calories 415; Protein 21 g; Carbohydrate 28 g; Fat 21 g; Cholesterol 80 mg; Sodium 910 mg

CINCINNATI-STYLE CHILE: For each serving, spoon about ¾ cup beef mixture over 1 cup hot cooked spaghetti. Sprinkle each serving with ¼ cup shredded Cheddar cheese and 2 tablespoons chopped onion. Top with sour cream if desired.

EASY CHILE CON CARNE: Increase chile powder to 2 tablespoons; omit cumin, oregano, cocoa and pepper sauce.

Tacos

Let people build their own tacos just the way they like them.

1½ pounds ground beef
1 envelope (1¼ ounces) taco seasoning
  mix
1 cup water
12 ready-to-serve taco shells
¾ cup shredded lettuce
¾ cup chopped tomato
¾ cup ripe olives
¾ cup chopped onion
1 cup shredded Cheddar cheese
Salsa if desired
Sour cream if desired

Heat oven to 350°. Cook and stir ground beef in large skillet until brown. Drain off fat. Stir in taco seasoning mix and water; heat to boiling. Reduce heat and simmer uncovered 15 to 20 minutes, stirring occasionally. While meat simmers, heat taco shells on ungreased baking sheet in oven 3 to 5 minutes.

Spoon ¼ cup meat mixture into each taco shell. Add 1 tablespoon each lettuce, tomato, olives, onion, and cheese. Top with salsa and sour cream if desired.   **6 servings**

PER SERVING: Calories 500; Protein 29 g; Carbohydrate 28 g; Fat 30 g; Cholesterol 85 mg; Sodium 1000 mg

Taco Casserole

1 pound ground beef
1 can (15 ounces) chile beans
1 can (8 ounces) tomato sauce
2 tablespoons taco sauce
2 to 4 teaspoons chile powder
1 teaspoon garlic powder
2 cups coarsely broken tortilla chips
1 cup sour cream
½ cup sliced green onions (with tops)
1 medium tomato, chopped (about
  ¾ cup)
1 cup shredded Cheddar or Monterey
  Jack cheese (4 ounces)

Heat oven to 350°. Cook ground beef in 10-inch skillet, stirring frequently, until brown; drain. Stir in beans, tomato sauce, taco sauce, chile powder and garlic powder. Heat to boiling, stirring occasionally.

Place tortilla chips in ungreased 2-quart casserole. Top with beef mixture. Spread with sour cream. Sprinkle with onions, tomato and cheese. Bake uncovered 20 to 30 minutes or until hot and bubbly. Arrange additional tortilla chips around edge of casserole. Serve with shredded lettuce, chile peppers and taco sauce if desired.   **6 servings**

PER SERVING: Calories 505; Protein 27 g; Carbohydrate 29 g; Fat 32 g; Cholesterol 90 mg; Sodium 750 mg

Taco Salad

For a low-fat variation, substitute ground turkey for the ground beef and nonfat yogurt for the Thousand Island dressing, and omit the avocado. You reduce the fat by more than 50 percent and the calories by about 35 percent!

Tortilla Shells (right)
1 pound ground beef
⅔ cup water
1 tablespoon chile powder
½ teaspoon salt
¼ teaspoon garlic powder
¼ teaspoon ground red pepper (cayenne)
1 can (15½ ounces) kidney beans, drained (reserve empty can)
1 medium head lettuce, torn into bite-size pieces (about 10 cups)
1 cup shredded Cheddar cheese (4 ounces)
⅔ cup sliced ripe olives
2 medium tomatoes, coarsely chopped
1 medium onion, chopped (about ½ cup)
¾ cup bottled Thousand Island dressing
1 avocado, thinly sliced
Sour cream

Prepare Tortilla Shells. Cook ground beef in 10-inch skillet, stirring occasionally, until brown; drain. Stir in water, chile powder, salt, garlic powder, red pepper and kidney beans. Heat to boiling; reduce heat. Simmer uncovered 15 minutes, stirring occasionally; cool 10 minutes.

Mix lettuce, cheese, olives, tomatoes and onion in large bowl. Toss with Thousand Island dressing. Pour ground beef mixture over top and toss. Divide among Tortilla Shells. Garnish with avocado and sour cream. Serve immediately.

8 servings

PER SERVING: Calories 610; Protein 22 g; Carbohydrate 31 g; Fat 46 g; Cholesterol 65 mg; Sodium 660 mg

MICROWAVE DIRECTIONS: Crumble ground beef into 2-quart microwavable casserole. Cover loosely and microwave on high 6 to 7 minutes, stirring after 3 minutes, until no pink remains; drain. Reduce water to ¼ cup. Stir in water, chile powder, salt, garlic powder, red pepper and kidney beans. Cover loosely and microwave on high 2 to 3 minutes or until boiling. Continue as directed.

How to Make Tortilla Shells

Remove label and both ends of kidney bean can; wash and dry. Heat 1½ inches vegetable oil in 3-quart saucepan to 375°. (Diameter of saucepan should be at least 9 inches.) Place 1 of 8 flour tortillas (10 inches in diameter) on top of saucepan; place can on center of tortilla with long-handled tongs. Push tortilla into oil by gently pushing can down. Fry tortilla until slightly set, about 5 seconds; remove can with tongs. Continue frying tortilla, turning tortilla in oil, until tortilla is crisp and golden brown, 1 to 2 minutes longer. Carefully remove tortilla from oil; drain excess oil from inside. Turn tortilla shell upside down; cool. Repeat with remaining tortillas.

To make ahead, cover cooled Tortilla Shells tightly and store at room temperature up to 24 hours.

Mexican Pizza

An old favorite gets a Mexican flavor.

Pizza Crust (right)
1 pound ground beef
1 large onion, chopped (about ¾ cup)
1 clove garlic, crushed
1 can (15 ounces) refried beans or Re-
friend Beans (page 20)
1 can (4 ounces) chopped green chiles,
drained
1 jar (8 ounces) taco sauce
2 cups shredded Monterey Jack or Cheddar cheese (8 ounces)
1 tablespoon sliced ripe olives

Heat oven to 450°. Prepare Pizza Crust; bake 5 minutes. Cook and stir ground beef, onion and garlic in 10-inch skillet over medium-high heat until beef is brown; drain. Spread beans to edge of baked crust. Layer beef mixture, chiles, taco sauce, cheese and olives on beans. Cover edge of crust with 2- to 3-inch strip of aluminum foil to prevent excessive browning. Bake 10 minutes; remove foil. Bake until crust is golden brown and cheese is bubbly in center, about 10 minutes longer. Serve with chopped tomatoes, sour cream and guacamole if desired.

6 servings

PER SERVING: Calories 620; Protein 34 g; Carbohy-drate 53 g; Fat 30 g; Cholesterol 115 mg; Sodium 1480 mg

Pizza Crust

1 package active dry yeast
½ cup warm water (105 to 115°)
1 teaspoon sugar
¾ teaspoon salt
1 egg
1½ teaspoons vegetable oil
2 to 2¼ cups all-purpose flour
Vegetable oil

Dissolve yeast in warm water in large bowl. Stir in sugar, salt, egg, 1½ teaspoons oil and 1 cup of the flour. Beat until smooth. Mix in enough remaining flour to make dough easy to handle. Turn dough onto lightly floured surface; knead until smooth, about 3 minutes. (Dough will be soft.) Cover and let rest 15 minutes.

Grease 12-inch pizza pan. Roll dough into 14-inch circle; fold into fourths. Place in pan. Unfold dough and ease into pan, forming 1-inch rim. (Or, instead of rolling, dough can be patted in pan with floured fingers.) Brush dough with oil.

Chile with Macaroni

1 pound ground beef
2 medium onions, chopped (about 1 cup)
1 large green bell pepper, chopped
  (about 1 cup)
1 can (28 ounces) whole tomatoes,
  undrained
1 can (15 ounces) kidney beans,
  undrained
1 can (8 ounces) tomato sauce
1 cup uncooked elbow macaroni (about 3
  ounces)
2 to 4 teaspoons chile powder
1 teaspoon salt
1/8 teaspoon ground red pepper
  (cayenne)
1/8 teaspoon paprika

Cook ground beef, onions and bell pepper in 10-inch skillet, stirring frequently, until beef is brown; drain. Stir in remaining ingredients; break up tomatoes. Heat to boiling; reduce heat. Cover and simmer 20 to 30 minutes, stirring occasionally, until macaroni is tender.   **6 servings**

PER SERVING: Calories 360; Protein 24 g; Carbohydrate 35 g; Fat 15 g; Cholesterol 65 mg; Sodium 1090 mg

Beef with Olives and Almonds

This dish, called picadillo *in Mexico, is a colorful mélange of ground beef, green pepper, tomato and pimiento-stuffed olive. It is seasoned with garlic and perfumed with cinnamon and cloves. Raisins and almonds are added treats to this minced meat hash, which often fills tortillas, pies and peppers.*

1 pound ground beef
1 medium onion, chopped (about 1/2 cup)
1 clove garlic, chopped
2 medium tomatoes, chopped
1 medium green bell pepper, chopped
1/4 cup raisins
1 1/2 teaspoons salt
1/8 teaspoon ground cinnamon
1/8 teaspoon ground cloves
1/4 cup slivered almonds
1/4 cup sliced pimiento-stuffed olives
Hot cooked rice

Cook and stir ground beef, onion and garlic in 10-inch skillet until beef is light brown; drain. Add tomatoes, bell pepper, raisins, salt, cinnamon and cloves. Cover and simmer 10 minutes.

Cook and stir almonds over medium heat until golden, 2 to 3 minutes. Stir almonds and olives into beef mixture. Serve with rice.

4 servings

PER SERVING: Calories 465; Protein 28 g; Carbohydrate 45 g; Fat 19 g; Cholesterol 70 mg; Sodium 1090 mg

Spicy Beef Burgers

1 pound ground beef
1 small onion, chopped (about ¼ cup)
2 to 3 tablespoons chopped green chiles
½ teaspoon salt
⅛ teaspoon pepper
1 medium clove garlic, chopped
4 hamburger buns
Chile-Cheese Spread (below)

Mix all ingredients except buns and Chile-Cheese Spread. Shape beef mixture into 4 patties, each about ½ inch thick. Cook in 10-inch skillet over medium heat, turning once, about 10 minutes for medium or until desired doneness. Serve on hamburger buns with Chile-Cheese Spread.   **4 servings**

PER SERVING: Calories 355; Protein 24 g; Carbohydrate 24 g; Fat 18 g; Cholesterol 65 mg; Sodium 540 mg

Chile–Cheese Spread

½ cup shredded Cheddar cheese
   (2 ounces)
2 tablespoons sour cream
2 tablespoons chopped green chiles

Mix all ingredients. Spread about 2 tablespoons mixture over each burger.

Pork Tenderloin in Tequila

¼ cup prepared mustard
2 pounds pork tenderloin
¼ cup vegetable oil
2 cloves garlic, cut into halves
¼ cup chopped carrot
¼ cup chopped celery
¼ cup lime juice
¼ cup tequila or lime juice
1 tablespoon ground red chiles
1 teaspoon salt
1 teaspoon dried oregano leaves
1 teaspoon dried thyme leaves
¼ teaspoon pepper
4 medium tomatoes, chopped (about
   4 cups)
1 small onion, chopped (about ¼ cup)
1 bay leaf
¼ cup snipped fresh parsley

Spread mustard over pork tenderloin. Heat oil and garlic in 10-inch skillet until hot. Cook pork in oil over medium heat until brown. Remove garlic.

Stir in remaining ingredients except parsley. Heat to boiling; reduce heat. Cover and simmer until pork is done, about 30 minutes. Remove bay leaf. Sprinkle with parsley.   **6 servings**

PER SERVING: Calories 365; Protein 45 g; Carbohydrate 8 g; Fat 17 g; Cholesterol 140 mg; Sodium 600 mg

Pork Tenderloin in Tequila

Pork Fajitas

Tortillas vary in size, weight and, of course, calories. When buying them by weight, select the package with the most tortillas; they'll be thinner and have fewer calories.

¾ **pound lean pork tenderloin**
1 **tablespoon vegetable oil**
2 **tablespoons lime juice**
2 **cloves garlic, sliced**
2 **teaspoons chile powder**
1 **teaspoon garlic powder**
½ **teaspoon salt**
¼ **teaspoon pepper**
4 **flour tortillas (8 inches in diameter)**
1 **medium onion, sliced**
1 **medium green or red bell pepper, cut into ¼-inch strips**
¾ **cup chopped seeded tomato (about 1 medium)**
¼ **cup reduced-calorie sour cream**

Trim fat from pork tenderloin; cut pork with grain into 2-inch strips. Cut strips across grain into ¼-inch slices. (For ease in cutting, partially freeze pork, about 1½ hours.) Mix 1 tablespoon oil, the lime juice, garlic, chile powder, garlic powder, salt and pepper in glass or plastic bowl or heavy plastic bag. Place pork in bowl, tossing to coat. Cover and refrigerate at least 8 hours but no longer than 24 hours, turning pork occasionally.

Heat oven to 350°. Wrap tortillas in aluminum foil and heat until warm, about 15 minutes. Remove from oven; keep tortillas wrapped. Remove pork from marinade.

Heat 10-inch nonstick skillet or wok over medium-high heat until 1 or 2 drops water bubble and skitter when sprinkled in skillet. Add pork; stir-fry 4 minutes. Add onion and bell pepper; stir-fry until vegetables are crisp-tender, 4 to 5 minutes longer.

For each serving, place one-fourth of the pork mixture, chopped tomato and sour cream in center of tortilla. Fold tortilla over filling; serve with lime wedges if desired.   **4 servings**

PER SERVING: Calories 300; Protein 19 g; Carbohydrate 30 g; Fat 12 g; Cholesterol 50 mg; Sodium 330 mg

Shredded Pork Tamales

18 **dried corn husks**
1 **small onion, chopped (about ¼ cup)**
2 **tablespoons vegetable oil**
¼ **cup Basic Red Sauce (page 12)**
Shredded Pork (right)
2 **tablespoons raisins**
2 **tablespoons capers**
2 **tablespoons snipped fresh cilantro**
Tamale Dough (right)
18 **pitted olives**

Cover corn husks with warm water and let stand until pliable, at least 2 hours. Cook and stir onion in oil in 3-quart saucepan until tender. Stir in Red Sauce, Shredded Pork and remaining ingredients except Tamale Dough and olives. Heat to boiling; reduce heat. Cover and cook 15 minutes. (If mixture is too dry, add a little reserved pork liquid.) Prepare Tamale Dough.

Drain corn husks; pat dry with paper towels.

Spread ¼ cup dough across center of each husk from 1 edge to within ½ inch of other edge.

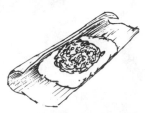

Spoon 2 tablespoons pork mixture into center of dough; top with 1 olive.

Roll husks around filling starting with dough edge.

Fold both ends up toward center. Secure with string if necessary.

Place tamales on rack in Dutch oven or steamer. Pour boiling water into Dutch oven to just under rack level. Cover Dutch oven. Keep water simmering over low heat 1 hour.   **18 tamales**

PER SERVING: Calories 295; Protein 9 g; Carbohydrate 17 g; Fat 21 g; Cholesterol 25 mg; Sodium 640 mg

Shredded Pork

1 pound pork boneless shoulder
1 tomato, chopped
1 small onion, cut into fourths
1 carrot, cut into 1-inch pieces
1 stalk celery, cut into 1-inch pieces
1 tablespoon chile powder
1 teaspoon salt
¼ teaspoon cumin seed
¼ teaspoon dried oregano leaves
¼ teaspoon pepper
1 clove garlic, crushed
1 bay leaf

Place all ingredients in 3-quart saucepan. Add enough water to cover. Heat to boiling; reduce heat. Cover and simmer until pork is tender, about 1½ hours. Drain; reserve 2 cups broth for Tamale Dough. Cool and shred pork.

Tamale Dough

1 cup shortening or lard
2 cups masa harina
3 teaspoons baking powder
1 teaspoon salt
2 cups reserved chicken broth

Beat all ingredients in large mixer bowl on low speed, scraping bowl constantly, until mixture forms a smooth paste. Beat on medium speed until light and fluffy, about 10 minutes.

Picante Pork Chile

Picante Pork Chile

1 medium onion, chopped (about ½ cup)
1 medium green bell pepper, chopped
  (about 1 cup)
1 clove garlic, finely chopped
½ pound ground pork
1 cup salsa or Fresh Tomato Salsa
  (page 11)
1 teaspoon chile powder
¼ teaspoon salt
1 can (16 ounces) pinto beans, rinsed
  and drained
1 can (16 ounces) whole tomatoes,
  undrained

Cook onion, bell pepper, garlic and pork in 3-quart saucepan over medium heat, stirring frequently, until pork is no longer pink; drain if necessary. Stir in remaining ingredients, breaking up tomatoes. Cover and simmer 10 minutes.

4 servings

PER SERVING: Calories 370; Protein 22 g; Carbohydrate 44 g; Fat 12 g; Cholesterol 35 mg; Sodium 1240 mg

Spicy Mexican Torte

½ pound chorizo sausage, casings
  removed
2 medium onions, chopped (about 1 cup)
2 cloves garlic, finely chopped
1 can (4 ounces) chopped green chiles,
  drained
8 flour tortillas (10 inches in diameter)
2 cups shredded Monterey Jack or hot
  pepper cheese (8 ounces)
1 can (16 ounces) refried beans or Refried Beans (page 20)
1 jar (7 ounces) roasted red peppers,
  drained

Cook sausage, onions and garlic in 10-inch skillet over medium heat, stirring occasionally, until sausage is done; drain. Stir in green chiles; set aside.

Heat oven to 400°. Grease pie plate, 10 × 1½ inches. Place 2 tortillas in pie plate. Spread half of the sausage mixture over tortillas. Sprinkle with half of the cheese. Place 2 tortillas on cheese. Spread with beans. Place 2 tortillas on beans and place peppers on tortillas. Place 2 tortillas on peppers. Spread with remaining sausage mixture. Sprinkle with remaining cheese. Cover and bake 40 minutes. Uncover and bake 15 minutes or until cheese is melted and center is hot. Cool 10 minutes before cutting. Serve with salsa, sour cream or guacamole if desired. **8 servings**

PER SERVING: Calories 350; Protein 15 g; Carbohydrate 30 g; Fat 17 g; Cholesterol 310 mg; Sodium 510 mg

NOTE: Sixteen 6-inch corn tortillas can be substituted for the flour tortillas. Overlap 4 tortillas for each layer.

Sausage in Corn Bread with Salsa–Sour Cream Sauce

A dish that uses corn bread in an unusual and tasty way.

1 pound pork sausage links
Corn Bread (page 25)
½ cup shredded process sharp American
  cheese (2 ounces)
3 medium green onions (with tops),
  chopped (about ¼ cup)
Salsa–Sour Cream Sauce (below)

Heat oven to 400°. Cook sausages in 10-inch ovenproof skillet as directed on package; drain. Prepare Corn Bread—except use ovenproof skillet and stir in cheese and onions. Pour batter into skillet. Arrange sausages in spoke fashion on top. Bake about 20 minutes or until corn bread is golden brown. Serve in wedges with Salsa–Sour Cream Sauce.   **6 servings**

PER SERVING: Calories 455; Protein 17 g; Carbohydrate 27 g; Fat 31 g; Cholesterol 145 mg; Sodium 1740 mg

Salsa–Sour Cream Sauce

2 cups prepared salsa
½ cup sour cream

Mix ingredients in 1-quart saucepan. Heat over medium heat until hot.

Spicy Sausage Burritos

Burritos or "little donkeys" are soft tortillas wrapped around refried beans and chile-flavored meat. For those who favor fiery food, serve with red pepper sauce.

Refried Beans (page 20)
1 pound bulk pork sausage
1 medium tomato, coarsely chopped
1 tablespoon chile powder
1 tablespoon vinegar
1 clove garlic, finely chopped
½ teaspoon salt
¼ teaspoon ground cinnamon
8 flour tortillas (10 inches in diameter)
1 cup shredded Monterey Jack cheese
  (4 ounces)

Prepare Refried Beans. Cook and stir pork sausage in 10-inch skillet until light brown; drain. Stir in tomato, chile powder, vinegar, garlic, salt and cinnamon. Heat to boiling; reduce heat. Simmer uncovered, stirring occasionally, until thickened, about 10 minutes.

Heat oven to 350°. Soften tortillas, one at a time, in ungreased hot skillet, about 30 seconds on each side. Spread about ⅓ cup refried beans over each hot tortilla. Spoon about ¼ cup sausage mixture onto center of tortilla; sprinkle with cheese. Fold up bottom of tortilla. Fold sides over and roll from bottom. Place tortillas, seam sides down, in ungreased jelly roll pan, 15½ × 10½ × 1 inch. Bake uncovered until hot, about 20 minutes.   **8 burritos**

PER SERVING: Calories 435; Protein 18 g; Carbohydrate 46 g; Fat 20 g; Cholesterol 45 mg; Sodium 940 mg

Enchiladas with Green Sauce

This Green Sauce—a Mexico City specialty—is made with spinach.

2 cups shredded Monterey Jack cheese
(8 ounces)
1 cup shredded Cheddar cheese
(4 ounces)
1 medium onion, chopped (about ½ cup)
½ cup sour cream
2 tablespoons snipped fresh parsley
½ teaspoon salt
¼ teaspoon pepper
Green Sauce (right)
8 tortillas (6 inches in diameter)

In a large bowl stir together cheeses, onion, sour cream, parsley, salt and pepper. Set aside.

Prepare Green Sauce. Heat tortillas, one at a time, in ungreased hot skillet until softened, about 30 seconds. (Cover hot tortillas to prevent drying.) Dip each tortilla into Green Sauce to coat both sides. Spoon about ¼ cup filling onto each tortilla; roll tortilla around filling.

Heat oven to 350°. Arrange enchiladas, seam sides down, in ungreased rectangular baking dish, 12 × 7½ × 2 inches. Pour remaining sauce over enchiladas. Bake uncovered until bubbly, about 20 minutes. Garnish with shredded Cheddar or Monterey Jack cheese and lime wedges if desired.   **4 servings**

PER SERVING: Calories 825; Protein 33 g; Carbohydrate 56 g; Fat 52 g; Cholesterol 135 mg; Sodium 1690 mg

Green Sauce

10 ounces spinach
2 tablespoons margarine or butter
2 tablespoons all-purpose flour
¼ teaspoon salt
½ cup milk
1½ cups chicken broth
1 to 2 tablespoons canned chopped green chiles
1 small onion, chopped (about ¼ cup)
1 clove garlic, finely chopped
¾ teaspoon ground cumin
⅔ cup sour cream

Wash spinach; cover and cook with just the water that clings to leaves until tender, 3 to 5 minutes. Drain and pat dry; chop coarsely.

Heat margarine over low heat until melted. Blend in flour and salt. Cook over low heat, stirring constantly, until smooth and bubbly; remove from heat. Stir in milk and ½ cup of the chicken broth. Heat to boiling, stirring constantly. Boil and stir 1 minute. Stir in remaining chicken broth. Cook and stir over low heat until hot; remove from heat. Stir in spinach and remaining ingredients.

_____

NOTE: 1 package (10 ounces) frozen chopped spinach, cooked and well drained, can be substituted for the fresh spinach.

Enchilada Casserole

2 cups shredded Monterey Jack cheese
   (8 ounces)
1 cup shredded Cheddar cheese
   (4 ounces)
1 medium onion, chopped (about ½ cup)
½ cup sour cream
2 tablespoons snipped fresh parsley
¼ teaspoon salt
¼ teaspoon pepper
1 can (15 ounces) tomato sauce
⅔ cup water
⅓ cup chopped green bell pepper
1 tablespoon chile powder
½ teaspoon dried oregano leaves
¼ teaspoon ground cumin
1 clove garlic, finely chopped
8 tortillas
¼ cup shredded Cheddar cheese
   (1 ounce)

Heat oven to 350°. Mix Monterey Jack cheese, 1 cup Cheddar cheese, the onion, sour cream, parsley, salt and pepper; reserve. Heat tomato sauce, water, bell pepper, chile powder, oregano, cumin and garlic to boiling, stirring occasionally; reduce heat. Simmer uncovered 5 minutes. Pour into ungreased pie plate, 8 or 9 × 1¼ inches.

Dip each tortilla into sauce to coat both sides. Spoon about ¼ cup cheese mixture onto each tortilla; roll tortilla around filling. Arrange in ungreased rectangular baking dish, 12 × 7½ × 2 inches. Pour remaining sauce over enchiladas. Sprinkle with ¼ cup Cheddar cheese. Bake uncovered until hot and bubbly, about 20 minutes. Garnish with sour cream and sliced olives or lime wedges if desired. **4 servings**

PER SERVING: Calories 730; Protein 31 g; Carbohydrate 60 g; Fat 41 g; Cholesterol 115 mg; Sodium 1710 mg

DO-AHEAD NOTE: After sprinkling with cheese, cover and refrigerate no longer than 24 hours. To serve, bake uncovered in 350° oven about 35 minutes.

Macaroni con Queso

Chile con Queso (below)
4 ounces uncooked elbow macaroni or
   macaroni shells (about 1 cup)
1 large tomato, chopped (about 1 cup)
1 tablespoon chopped fresh cilantro
   leaves
1 cup shredded Cheddar or Monterey
   Jack cheese (4 ounces)
¼ cup crushed tortilla chips

Heat oven to 375°. Prepare Chile con Queso. Cook macaroni as directed on package; drain. Mix macaroni, Chile con Queso, tomato and cilantro in ungreased 1½-quart casserole. Sprinkle with cheese and tortilla chips. Bake uncovered about 30 minutes or until hot and bubbly.

4 servings

PER SERVING: Calories 395; Protein 19 g; Carbohydrate 28 g; Fat 23 g; Cholesterol 70 mg; Sodium 700 mg

Chile con Queso

1 cup shredded Cheddar or Monterey Jack
   cheese (4 ounces)
1 or 2 jalapeño chiles, seeded and finely
   chopped
½ cup milk
¼ cup half-and-half
2 tablespoons finely chopped onion
2 teaspoons ground cumin
½ teaspoon salt

Heat all ingredients over low heat, stirring constantly, until cheese is melted.

Tex-Mex Scrambled Eggs

6 corn tortillas (6 inches in diameter)
3 tablespoons vegetable oil
½ cup chopped green onions (with tops)
6 eggs, beaten
1 cup cubed Mexican-style process
  cheese spread with jalapeño chiles
  (about 4 ounces)
1 medium tomato, chopped

Cut each tortilla into 12 wedges. Heat oil in 10-inch skillet just until hot. Cook tortilla wedges in oil over medium-high heat, stirring frequently, until crisp; reduce heat. Add onions. Cook and stir over medium heat 1 minute.

Pour eggs over tortilla mixture. As eggs begin to set at bottom and side, gently lift cooked portions with spatula so that thin, uncooked portion can flow to bottom. Do not stir. Sprinkle with cheese. Cook 1 to 2 minutes longer or until cheese is melted and eggs are thickened throughout but still moist. Top with tomato. Sprinkle with chopped cilantro, oregano or parsley if desired. **4 servings**

PER SERVING: Calories 370; Protein 18 g; Carbohydrate 17 g; Fat 25 g; Cholesterol 410 mg; Sodium 555 mg

Potato Omelet

¾ cup olive oil
4 medium potatoes, pared and cut into
  ⅛-inch slices (about 1½ pounds)
1 medium onion, cut into ⅛-inch slices
4 eggs
½ teaspoon salt
¼ teaspoon pepper

Heat oil in 10-inch nonstick skillet until hot; layer potato and onion slices alternately in skillet. Cook over medium-low heat, turning frequently, until potatoes are tender but not brown, about 12 minutes. Remove potatoes and onion with slotted spoon; drain, reserving 3 tablespoons oil in skillet.

Beat eggs, ¼ teaspoon of the salt and the pepper in large bowl; gently stir in potatoes and onion. Sprinkle remaining salt over potatoes. Heat oil in skillet until hot; pour egg and potato mixture into skillet. Cook uncovered over medium-low heat until potatoes begin to brown on bottom and edge of omelet is firm (center will be wet), about 7 minutes. (Shake pan occasionally to prevent omelet from sticking.) Place large plate over skillet; invert omelet onto plate. Slide omelet back into skillet. Continue to cook over medium-low heat until eggs are set and potatoes are golden brown, about 2 minutes longer. Turn onto serving plate; cut into wedges.

4 servings

PER SERVING: Calories 290; Protein 8 g; Carbohydrate 22 g; Fat 19 g; Cholesterol 215 mg; Sodium 340 mg

Cheese

Cheese became a distinctive ingredient in Mexican cooking with the introduction of cows and goats by the Spaniards. Many varieties are used for stuffing, layering and topping in recipes.

Store cheese in the refrigerator. Wrap it tightly in aluminum foil or plastic wrap to prevent moisture loss. Firm cheeses such as Cheddar keep two months or more; semisoft cheeses such as Monterey Jack keep about 3 weeks and soft cheeses such as cream cheese, about 2 weeks. If mold forms on cheese other than Roquefort and blue cheeses, which are mold-ripened, cut it off. If mold has penetrated cheese, discard the cheese. Freeze slices and pieces of cheese tightly wrapped in moisture-proof freezer wrap for up to 3 months. Thaw in refrigerator rather than at room temperature to prevent excessive crumbling.

Ranch-style Eggs

Strictly speaking, huevos rancheros *means any Mexican egg dish made with tortillas. This, the most popular version, serves up fried eggs on corn tortillas with a topping of tomato–green chile sauce.*

Mexican Sauce (right)
Vegetable oil
8 corn tortillas (4 inches in diameter)
Vegetable oil
8 eggs
Salt and pepper
1 cup shredded Monterey Jack cheese
   (4 ounces)

Prepare Mexican Sauce. Heat oil (1/8 inch) in 6- or 8-inch skillet until hot. Cook tortillas until crisp and light brown, about 1 minute on each side. Drain; keep warm.

Heat oil (1/8 inch) in 12-inch skillet until hot. Break each egg into measuring cup or saucer; carefully slip 4 eggs, 1 at a time, into skillet. Immediately reduce heat. Cook slowly, spooning oil over eggs until whites are set and a film forms over the yolks. (Or, turn eggs over gently when whites are set and cook to desired doneness.) Sprinkle with salt and pepper. Repeat with remaining eggs.

Spoon 1 tablespoon sauce over each tortilla; place 1 egg on each. Spoon sauce over white of eggs; sprinkle yolks with cheese.

4 servings

PER SERVING: Calories 520; Protein 23 g; Carbohydrate 24 g; Fat 37 g; Cholesterol 450 mg; Sodium 500 mg

Mexican Sauce

1 medium onion, chopped (about 1/2 cup)
1/2 medium green bell pepper, chopped
1 clove garlic, finely chopped
1 tablespoon vegetable oil
2 cups chopped ripe tomatoes
1/4 to 1/2 cup chopped green chiles
5 drops red pepper sauce
1/2 teaspoon sugar
1/8 teaspoon salt

Cook and stir onion, bell pepper and garlic in oil in 2-quart saucepan until bell pepper is tender, about 5 minutes. Stir in remaining ingredients. Heat to boiling; reduce heat. Simmer uncovered until slightly thickened, about 15 minutes.

NOTE: 1 can (16 ounces) tomatoes (with liquid) can be substituted for the ripe tomatoes. Break up tomatoes with fork.

Spicy Black Bean Burritos

Pumpkin Seed Sauce (right)
1 cup chopped broccoli
1/2 cup chopped onion (about 1 medium)
2 cloves garlic, finely chopped
1 tablespoon reduced-calorie margarine
1 can (15 ounces) black beans, drained
1 cup julienne strips yellow squash
   (about 1 medium)
1 small red bell pepper, cut into
   2 × 1/4-inch strips
2 tablespoons shelled pumpkin seeds,
   toasted
1 tablespoon lemon juice
1/4 teaspoon red pepper flakes
1/4 teaspoon ground cumin
6 flour tortillas (about 8 inches in diameter), warmed

Prepare Pumpkin Seed Sauce; keep warm. Cook broccoli, onion and garlic in margarine in

10-inch nonstick skillet, stirring frequently, until onion is softened. Stir in remaining ingredients except tortillas. Cook uncovered, stirring occasionally, until squash and bell pepper are crisp-tender.

Spoon about ½ cup of the vegetable mixture onto center of each tortilla. Fold one end of tortilla up about 1 inch over mixture; fold right and left sides over, overlapping. Fold remaining end down. Serve with Pumpkin Seed Sauce.

PER SERVING: Calories 265; Protein 13 g; Carbohydrate 37 g; Fat 8 g; Cholesterol 0 mg; Sodium 180 mg

6 servings

Pumpkin Seed Sauce

  2 tablespoons chopped onion
  1 small clove garlic, crushed
  1 tablespoon reduced-calorie margarine
  2 tablespoons shelled pumpkin seeds
  1 slice whole wheat bread, torn into small
    pieces
  1 tablespoon canned chopped green
    chiles
  ¼ cup chicken broth
  ¼ cup evaporated skim milk
  Dash of salt

Cook onion and garlic in margarine, stirring frequently, until onion is softened. Stir in pumpkin seeds and bread. Cook over medium heat, stirring frequently, until bread is golden brown. Stir in chiles. Place mixture in blender or food processor. Cover and blend or process until finely ground. Add broth, milk and salt. Cover and process until blended.

Bean and Cheese Tacos

Red Salsa (below)
1 can (8 ounces) kidney beans, drained
  (reserve liquid)
1 clove garlic, finely chopped
4 flour tortillas (8 inches in diameter)
1 cup part skim ricotta cheese (8 ounces)
¼ cup grated Parmesan cheese
¼ cup chopped green onions (with tops)
1 tablespoon chopped fresh or 1 teaspoon dried cilantro leaves

Prepare Red Salsa. Heat oven to 350°. Mash beans and garlic. (Add 1 to 2 tablespoons reserved bean liquid if beans are dry.) Place tortillas on ungreased cookie sheet. Spread about ¼ cup of the bean mixture on half of each tortilla to within ½ inch of edge. Mix cheeses, onions and cilantro; spread over beans. Fold tortillas over filling. Bake until tortillas begin to brown and filling is hot, about 10 minutes. Serve with Red Salsa. **4 servings**

PER SERVING: Calories 300; Protein 16 g; Carbohydrate 38 g; Fat 10 g; Cholesterol 25 mg; Sodium 110 mg

Red Salsa

  1 large clove garlic, finely chopped
  1 cup chopped tomato (about 1 medium)
  ¼ cup chopped green onions (with tops)
  2 to 3 teaspoons chopped jalapeño chile
    (about ½ small)
  1½ teaspoons finely snipped fresh cilan-
    tro, if desired
  1½ teaspoons lemon juice
  1 teaspoon snipped fresh or ½ teaspoon
    dried oregano leaves

Mix all ingredients; cover and refrigerate at least 1 hour.

Bean–Cheese Pie

Bean–Cheese Pie

¾ cup all-purpose flour
½ cup shredded Cheddar cheese
(2 ounces)
1½ teaspoons baking powder
½ teaspoon salt
⅓ cup milk
1 egg, slightly beaten
1 can (15½ ounces) garbanzo beans,
drained
1 can (15 ounces) kidney beans, drained
1 can (8 ounces) tomato sauce
½ cup chopped green bell pepper (about
1 small)
¼ cup chopped onion (about 1 small)
2 teaspoons chile powder
2 teaspoons fresh or ½ teaspoon dried
oregano leaves
¼ teaspoon garlic powder
½ cup shredded Cheddar cheese
(2 ounces)

Heat oven to 375°. Spray pie plate, 10 × 1½ inches, with nonstick cooking spray. Mix flour, ½ cup cheese, the baking powder and salt in medium bowl. Stir in milk and egg until blended. Spread over bottom and up side of pie plate. Mix remaining ingredients except ½ cup cheese. Spoon into pie plate; sprinkle with ½ cup cheese. Bake uncovered about 25 minutes or until edge is puffy and light brown. Let stand 10 minutes before cutting. **8 servings**

PER SERVING: Calories 315; Protein 18 g; Carbohydrate 40 g; Fat 11 g; Cholesterol 50 mg; Sodium 730 mg

Impossible Chile–Cheese Pie

A pie that makes its own crust!

2 cans (4 ounces each) chopped green
chiles, drained
4 cups shredded Cheddar cheese
(16 ounces)
2 cups milk
4 eggs
1 cup Bisquick® original baking mix

Heat oven to 425°. Grease pie plate, 10 × 1½ inches. Sprinkle chiles and cheese in pie plate. Place remaining ingredients in blender. Cover and blend on high speed about 15 seconds or until smooth. (Or beat remaining ingredients on high speed 1 minute.) Pour into pie plate. Bake 25 to 30 minutes or until knife inserted in center comes out clean. Cool 10 minutes.

8 servings

PER SERVING: Calories 000; Protein 20 g; Carbohydrate 14 g; Fat 25 g; Cholesterol 200 mg; Sodium 595 mg

MICROWAVE DIRECTIONS: Do not grease pie plate. Decrease milk to 1½ cups. Prepare as directed. Elevate pie plate on inverted microwavable dinner plate in microwave oven. Microwave uncovered on medium-high (70%) 12 to 18 minutes, rotating pie plate ¼ turn every 6 minutes, until knife inserted in center comes out clean. Cool 10 minutes.

Natillas

5

South-of-the-Border Desserts

Natillas

Natillas *are a version of floating island: little meringues set adrift on a pool of thin custard. Just before serving, run the dessert under the broiler for a pretty, golden effect.*

4 eggs, separated
½ teaspoon cream of tartar
1 cup granulated sugar
4 cups milk
½ cup granulated sugar
1 teaspoon vanilla
¼ teaspoon salt
⅛ teaspoon ground cinnamon
Powdered sugar, sifted

Beat egg whites and cream of tartar in a small bowl until foamy. Beat in 1 cup granulated sugar, 1 tablespoon at a time; continue beating until stiff and glossy. Do not underbeat.

Heat milk to simmering in 10-inch skillet over medium heat; reduce heat just until bubbles form around edge of skillet. Drop 12 mounds of egg white mixture, 3 or 4 at a time, into hot milk. Cook uncovered 2 minutes; turn gently. Cook uncovered 2 minutes longer. Remove meringues with slotted spoon and drain.

Strain milk; reserve 2¼ cups. Mix egg yolks, ½ cup granulated sugar, the vanilla, salt and cinnamon in heavy 2-quart nonaluminum saucepan.

Gradually stir in reserved milk. Cook over low heat, stirring constantly, until mixture coats a metal spoon, about 20 minutes. Remove from heat; place saucepan in cold water, stirring occasionally, until cool.

Place meringues in shallow 3-quart nonaluminum casserole. Pour custard over meringues; refrigerate 1 hour.

Just before serving, set oven control to broil. Sprinkle custard and meringues with powdered sugar. Broil with tops of meringues about 4 inches from heat until light brown, about 2 minutes. Refrigerate any remaining dessert.

6 servings

PER SERVING: Calories 320; Protein 9 g; Carbohydrate 58 g; Fat 6 g; Cholesterol 155 mg; Sodium 230 mg

Mango with Passion Fruit

1 large mango (about 1 pound), thinly
  sliced
8 pitted dates, cut into halves
1 passion fruit
½ cup vanilla yogurt or sour cream

Arrange mango and dates on 4 dessert plates.
Cut passion fruit into halves and scoop out center. Mix passion fruit and yogurt. Serve with
fruit.   **4 servings**

PER SERVING: Calories 110; Protein 2 g; Carbohydrate 23 g; Fat 1 g; Cholesterol 0 mg; Sodium 20 mg

Flan

*It seems that most cuisines have their ver-
sion of flan. In Mexico it is sometimes flavored with toasted coconut. Cooking the
custard in a water bath maintains even,
moist heat, which helps to cook the eggs
gently without danger of curdling.*

½ cup sugar
3 eggs, slightly beaten
1 can (12 ounces) evaporated milk
  (1⅔ cups)
⅓ cup sugar
2 teaspoons vanilla
⅛ teaspoon salt

Heat ½ cup sugar in heavy 1-quart saucepan
over low heat, stirring constantly, until melted
and golden brown. Divide syrup among four 6-
ounce custard cups; rotate cups to coat bottoms.
Allow syrup to harden in cups, about 5 minutes.

Heat oven to 350°. Mix remaining ingredients;
pour into custard cups. Place cups in square
pan, 9 × 9 × 2 inches, on oven rack. Pour very
hot water into pan to within ½ inch of tops of
cups. Bake until knife inserted halfway between

About Mangoes

Mangoes are cultivated in the warm cli-
mates of California, Mexico and Hawaii.
They are either rounded in shape or elongated and flattened. They vary in color
from green to a reddish tinge and have brilliant, orange-yellow pulp. A ripe mango
yields to gentle pressure of the fingers. If
it is firm to the touch, allow it to ripen at
room temperature; when ripe, store it in the
refrigerator.

Mangoes are usually eaten raw, and have
a sweet but slightly tart flavor, rather like a
cross between a pineapple and a peach.
They are as juicy as they are flavorful.

Score into fourths.

*Sliced peeled fruit lengthwise
close to the seed.*

To prepare a mango, score the skin in
fourths with a knife and peel like a banana.
Slice the peeled mango lengthwise just
above the seed with a sharp knife.

center and edge comes out clean, 40 to 50 minutes. Immediately remove from water. Unmold
and serve warm, or refrigerate and unmold at
serving time.   **4 servings**

PER SERVING: Calories 330; Protein 12 g; Carbohydrate 52 g; Fat 8 g; Cholesterol 175 mg; Sodium 230 mg

Pumpkin Flan

An interesting variation to flan.

¾ **cup sugar**
¼ **cup water**
1 **cup canned pumpkin**
¾ **cup sugar**
1 **teaspoon ground cinnamon**
½ **teaspoon ground ginger**
¼ **teaspoon ground allspice**
¼ **teaspoon ground nutmeg**
6 **eggs**
1 **cup half-and-half**
1 **cup whipping (heavy) cream**

Heat oven to 350°. Heat ¾ cup sugar and ¼ cup water to boiling in heavy 2-quart saucepan over low heat, stirring constantly. Boil, without stirring, until syrup is deep golden brown.

Place quiche dish, 9 × 1½ or 10 × 1¼ inches, in hot water until warm (to prevent dish from cracking when pouring hot syrup into it); dry completely. Pour syrup into dish; immediately rotate dish until syrup covers bottom.

Beat remaining ingredients except half-and-half and whipping cream in large bowl until well blended. Beat in half-and-half and whipping cream. Pour over syrup. Place dish in shallow roasting pan on oven rack. Pour very hot water into pan until 1 inch deep. Bake 1 to 1¼ hours or until knife inserted in center comes out clean.

Remove dish from water; cool 15 minutes. Refrigerate about 3 hours or until chilled. Loosen side of flan from dish, using knife; unmold. Refrigerate any remaining flan.   **12 servings**

PER SERVING: Calories 280; Protein 5 g; Carbohydrate 33 g; Fat 15 g; Cholesterol 170 mg; Sodium 60 mg

Mexican Honey Puffs

Sopaipillas—honey puffs—are named for the little pillows they resemble.

1 **tablespoon shortening**
2 **cups all-purpose flour**
1 **teaspoon baking powder**
½ **teaspoon salt**
⅔ to ¾ **cup cold water**
Vegetable oil
Honey Butter or Cinnamon Sugar (below)

Cut shortening into flour, baking powder and salt until mixture resembles fine crumbs. Gradually add enough water to make a stiff dough, tossing with fork until all flour is moistened and dough almost cleans side of bowl. Gather dough into a ball; divide into halves and shape into 2 flattened rounds. Cover half to prevent drying.

Heat oil (1½ to 2 inches) to 360°. Roll 1 half of dough ⅛ to ¼ inch thick. Cut into rectangles, 3 × 2 inches, or 3-inch diamonds.

Fry 3 to 4 rectangles at a time, turning once, until puffed and golden brown, 1 to 2 minutes on each side; drain. Repeat with remaining dough.

Dip puffs into Honey Butter or sprinkle with Cinnamon Sugar.   **About 20 puffs**

PER SERVING: Calories 105; Protein 1 g; Carbohydrate 14 g; Fat 5 g; Cholesterol 0 mg; Sodium 90 mg

Honey Butter

⅓ **cup honey**
2 **tablespoons margarine or butter**

Heat honey and margarine until hot.

Cinnamon Sugar

3 **tablespoons sugar**
¼ **teaspoon ground cinnamon**

Mix sugar and cinnamon.

Biscochitos and Piñon Candy

Biscochitos

Biscochitos *are Mexico's answer to the Old World seed cookie. Rich with the flavor of anise, these holiday cookies were cut into* fleur de lis *shapes for Christmas.* Biscochitos *are quite short—traditionally a high ratio of lard to flour and sugar—and are as easy to roll out and cut as sugar cookies.*

1 cup sugar
1 cup margarine or butter, softened
3 tablespoons sweet sherry
1 egg
3 cups all-purpose flour
2 teaspoons baking powder
2 teaspoons anise seed, crushed
¼ teaspoon salt
¼ cup sugar
1 teaspoon ground cinnamon

Heat oven to 350°. Mix 1 cup sugar, margarine, sherry and egg in large bowl. Stir in remaining ingredients except ¼ cup sugar and the cinnamon. Divide dough into halves. Roll each half ¼ inch thick on lightly floured board.

Cut into desired shapes with cookie cutters; place on ungreased cookie sheet. Mix ¼ cup sugar and the cinnamon; sprinkle on cookies. Bake until light golden brown, 10 to 12 minutes. **About 4 dozen 2-inch cookies**

PER SERVING: Calories 85; Protein 1 g; Carbohydrate 11 g; Fat 4 g; Cholesterol 5 mg; Sodium 70 mg

Piñon Candy

2 cones piloncillo, shredded (about 1¼ cups), or 1 cup packed dark brown sugar
1 cup water
2 tablespoons butter
1½ cups toasted pine nuts or pecan halves
1 teaspoon vanilla

Heat piloncillo and water to boiling in 2-quart saucepan, stirring constantly; reduce heat slightly. Cook, without stirring, to 236° on candy thermometer or until small amount of mixture dropped into very cold water forms a soft ball that flattens when removed from water; remove from heat. Immediately remove thermometer; stir in butter. Cool 8 minutes without stirring.

Stir in pine nuts and vanilla. Beat with spoon until slightly thickened and mixture just coats pine nuts but remains glossy, about 1 minute. Drop by rounded teaspoonfuls onto waxed paper. Let stand until candies are firm. Store tightly covered at room temperature.

About 24 candies

PER SERVING: Calories 100; Protein 1 g; Carbohydrate 10 g; Fat 6 g; Cholesterol 5 mg; Sodium 15 mg

NOTE: Margarine not recommended.

NOTE: To toast nuts, spread them in a single layer in an ungreased pan; bake at 350°, stirring and checking for doneness frequently. Nuts are toasted when they are light brown. Pecans should bake for approximately 7 to 12 minutes, pine nuts for 5 to 7.

Lemon Fruit Tart

Lemon Fruit Tart

A soothing pecan crust filled with lemon mousse and topped with fresh fruit: a perfect contrast to a spicy Mexican meal.

Pecan Crust (right)
1 teaspoon unflavored gelatin
1 tablespoon cold water
½ cup sugar
2 eggs
2 tablespoons grated lemon peel
¼ cup lemon juice
½ cup whipping (heavy) cream
1 cup strawberry halves
1 cup raspberries
½ cup blackberries or blueberries
1 mango or papaya, pared and sliced
⅓ cup guava jelly or apricot jam, melted

Prepare Pecan Crust; cool. Sprinkle gelatin on cold water in 1½-quart saucepan to soften. Beat sugar and eggs until thick and lemon colored; stir into gelatin mixture. Heat just to boiling over low heat, stirring constantly, about 15 minutes. Remove from heat; stir in lemon peel and juice.

Beat whipping cream in chilled medium bowl until soft peaks form. Fold in lemon mixture; pour into Pecan Crust. Refrigerate 2 hours. Arrange fruits on top; drizzle with jelly. Refrigerate any remaining tart.   **8 servings**

PER SERVING: Calories 385; Protein 6 g; Carbohydrate 50 g; Fat 18 g; Cholesterol 95 mg; Sodium 100 mg

Pecan Crust

1 cup all-purpose flour
½ cup finely chopped pecans
¼ cup sugar
¼ cup margarine or butter, softened (½ stick)
1 egg

Heat oven to 375°. Mix flour, pecans and sugar; mix in margarine and egg until crumbly. Press in bottom and up side of greased tart pan, 9 × 1 inch. Bake until light golden brown, 15 to 20 minutes.

Mexican Desserts

The original dessert in Mexican cuisine was fresh fruit such as pineapple, oranges, strawberries, mangoes, papaya, bananas and melons, which grow in abundance. With the introduction of sugarcane into Mexico, a variety of puddings, custards and pastries flavored with cinnamon, almond, caramel, fruit or cheese became popular. Invented or adapted from French and Spanish desserts, they were eaten in celebration of feast days. Today, small servings are often served at the end of a meal and more often are eaten between meals. *Flan* is a nationwide favorite with recipes varying from region to region. Other desserts are pastries like the deep-fried Mexican Honey Puffs (*sopaipillas.*)

Chocolate–Cinnamon Cake Roll

Mexican cooks are fond of pairing chocolate with cinnamon; in fact, some brands of Mexican chocolate are flavored with cinnamon.

3 eggs
1 cup sugar
⅓ cup water
1 teaspoon coffee-flavored liqueur or
¾ cup all-purpose flour or 1 cup cake flour
¼ cup cocoa
1 teaspoon baking powder
¼ teaspoon salt
Cocoa
2 tablespoons coffee-flavored liqueur or coffee
Cinnamon Whipped Cream (right)

Heat oven to 375°. Line jelly roll pan, 15½ × 10½ × 1 inch, with aluminum foil or waxed paper; grease generously. Beat eggs in small mixer bowl on high speed until thick and lemon colored, about 5 minutes; pour into large mixer bowl. Gradually beat in sugar. Beat in water and 1 teaspoon liqueur on low speed. Gradually add flour, ¼ cup cocoa, the baking powder and salt, beating just until batter is smooth. Pour into pan.

Bake until wooden pick inserted in center comes out clean, 12 to 15 minutes. Immediately loosen cake from edges of pan; invert on towel sprinkled generously with cocoa. Carefully remove foil. Trim off stiff edges of cake if necessary.

While hot, carefully roll cake and towel from narrow end. Cool on wire rack at least 30 minutes. Unroll cake; remove towel. Sprinkle 2 tablespoons liqueur over cake. Spread with Cinnamon Whipped Cream; roll up. Sprinkle with cocoa if desired. Refrigerate until serving time. **10 servings**

PER SERVING: Calories 235; Protein 4 g; Carbohydrate 34 g; Fat 9 g; Cholesterol 90 mg; Sodium 120 mg

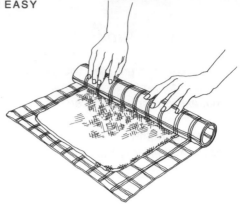

Gently roll hot cake and towel together from narrow end.

Cinnamon Whipped Cream

1 cup chilled whipping (heavy) cream
3 tablespoons powdered sugar
1 tablespoon coffee-flavored liqueur or coffee
1 teaspoon ground cinnamon

Beat all ingredients in chilled bowl until stiff.

Mexican Sundaes

1 tablespoon sugar
2 tablespoons instant cinnamon-flavored international coffee mix
1 tablespoon cocoa
1 teaspoon cornstarch
1 can (5 ounces) evaporated milk
1 pint coffee ice cream

Mix sugar, coffee mix (dry), cocoa and cornstarch in 1-quart saucepan. Gradually stir in milk. Heat over medium heat, stirring constantly, until mixture thickens and boils. Boil and stir 1 minute; remove from heat. Cool slightly. Press plastic wrap or waxed paper onto surface. Let stand about 30 minutes.

Spoon ice cream into dessert dishes. Top with warm sauce. **4 servings**

PER SERVING: Calories 220; Protein 5 g; Carbohydrate 28 g; Fat 10 g; Cholesterol 35 mg; Sodium 135 mg

Strawberry Margarita Pie

Graham Cracker Shell (below)
2 envelopes unflavored gelatin
1/2 cup water
3 cups strawberries
1/3 cup sugar
1/4 cup tequila or lime juice
1 tablespoon orange-flavored liqueur or
   orange juice
1/2 package (2.8-ounce size) whipped topping mix (1 envelope)

Prepare Graham Cracker Shell. Sprinkle gelatin on water in 2-quart saucepan. Let stand 1 minute to soften. Place strawberries, sugar, tequila and liqueur in blender or food processor. Cover and blend or process until smooth. Stir 1 cup strawberry mixture into gelatin mixture in saucepan. Heat over low heat 3 to 5 minutes, stirring constantly, until gelatin is dissolved. Stir in remaining strawberry mixture. Place pan in bowl of ice and water, or refrigerate 30 to 40 minutes, stirring occasionally, just until mixture mounds slightly when dropped from spoon.

Prepare topping mix in large bowl as directed on package—except omit vanilla and substitute skim milk for the milk. Fold strawberry mixture into whipped topping. Spoon into pie shell. Sprinkle with reserved crumb mixture from shell. Refrigerate about 2 hours or until set.

8 servings

PER SERVING: Calories 180; Protein 3 g; Carbohydrate 30 g; Fat 5 g; Cholesterol 0 mg; Sodium 115 mg

Graham Cracker Shell

1 1/4 cups graham cracker crumbs
2 tablespoons strawberry jelly
1 tablespoon vegetable oil

Spray pie plate, 9 × 1 1/4 inches, with nonstick cooking spray. Mix all ingredients. Reserve 2 tablespoons mixture for topping. Press remaining mixture firmly against bottom and side of pie plate.

Easy Mexican Chocolate Torte

2 cups chocolate fudge frosting mix
1/2 teaspoon ground cinnamon
2 cups chilled whipping (heavy) cream
33 graham crackers (each 2 1/2 inches
   square)
Chocolate Curls (below), if desired

Blend frosting mix (dry), cinnamon and whipping cream in chilled large bowl on low speed, scraping bowl constantly, 30 seconds. Beat on high speed until stiff, 2 to 3 minutes. Place small amount of frosting mixture on 3 crackers; arrange crackers on serving plate, frosting sides down, to form rectangle. Spread rectangle with about 1/4 cup frosting mixture; layer with 3 crackers. Repeat layers 9 times. Gently press torte together. Using pancake turners, carefully turn torte on its side so crackers are vertical. Frost top and sides with remaining frosting mixture. Decorate with Chocolate Curls. Refrigerate at least 6 hours (torte will mellow and become moist).

8 servings

PER SERVING: Calories 445; Protein 4 g; Carbohydrate 56 g; Fat 23 g; Cholesterol 70 mg; Sodium 220 mg

Chocolate Curls

Place bar of milk chocolate on waxed paper. (Curls will be easier to make if the chocolate is slightly warm. Let chocolate stand in warm place about 15 minutes.) Make curls by pressing a vegetable parer firmly against chocolate and pulling parer toward you in long, thin strokes.

METRIC CONVERSION GUIDE

U.S. UNITS	CANADIAN METRIC	AUSTRALIAN METRIC
Volume		
1/4 teaspoon	1 mL	1 ml
1/2 teaspoon	2 mL	2 ml
1 teaspoon	5 mL	5 ml
1 tablespoon	15 mL	20 ml
1/4 cup	50 mL	60 ml
1/3 cup	75 mL	80 ml
1/2 cup	125 mL	125 ml
2/3 cup	150 mL	170 ml
3/4 cup	175 mL	190 ml
1 cup	250 mL	250 ml
1 quart	1 liter	1 liter
1 1/2 quarts	1.5 liter	1.5 liter
2 quarts	2 liters	2 liters
2 1/2 quarts	2.5 liters	2.5 liters
3 quarts	3 liters	3 liters
4 quarts	4 liters	4 liters
Weight		
1 ounce	30 grams	30 grams
2 ounces	55 grams	60 grams
3 ounces	85 grams	90 grams
4 ounces (1/4 pound)	115 grams	125 grams
8 ounces (1/2 pound)	225 grams	225 grams
16 ounces (1 pound)	455 grams	500 grams
1 pound	455 grams	1/2 kilogram

Measurements

Inches	Centimeters
1	2.5
2	5.0
3	7.5
4	10.0
5	12.5
6	15.0
7	17.5
8	20.5
9	23.0
10	25.5
11	28.0
12	30.5
13	33.0
14	35.5
15	38.0

Temperatures

Fahrenheit	Celsius
32°	0°
212°	100°
250°	120°
275°	140°
300°	150°
325°	160°
350°	180°
375°	190°
400°	200°
425°	220°
450°	230°
475°	240°
500°	260°

NOTE
The recipes in this cookbook have not been developed or tested using metric measures. When converting recipes to metric, some variations in quality may be noted.

Index